KING JAMES ONLY?

Dr. Robert A. Joyner, D.B.S, Th.D, Ph.D

Published 1999 by
Dr. Robert A. Joyner

First printing, December 1999

To order additional copies of this book send check or money order to:

Dr Robert Joyner
760 Tom Mann Road
Newport, NC 28570

Single copy	$7.00
10 - 100	$6.00 each
over 100	$5.00 each

Price includes postage

Visit our church's webpage at: www.communitybaptistchurch.com
Email: info@communitybaptistchurch.com

TABLE OF CONTENTS

INTRODUCTION

God gloriously saved me 44 years ago at age 21. He called me to preach about 2 years later. I became an Independent Baptist just a few months after I was converted. I was in another denomination at the time. After diligent study of the Bible, I was convinced that Independent Baptist was the right way to go. I have never changed. I am almost 65 years old now (at the writing of this book).

I want to help Independent Baptists and all others that I can. This book is written with a sincere desire to be a blessing. I really believe it will help all who will read it with an open mind. It will teach you some things about God's Word and about the issue we are discussing.

This book deals with surface truth, obvious truth. I purposely do not go into tedious deep details. I do not think those things are necessary to find out the truth about the issue presented here.

Sometimes you cannot see the forest for the trees. Most of the time the King James Only debate gets bogged down in discussions about details the average Christian knows little about and is not interested in. In most books on this subject they discuss Dean Burgon, Origen, heretics in church history, scholars on both sides, Hebrew and Greek, Vaticanus and Alexandrian manuscripts, Westcott and Hort, etc. In this book you will find very little of this. What you will find is a clearer, easier to understand, concise discussion of the obvious facts. This book is written for the layman, not the scholar.

I believe the old saying, "The proof of the pudding is in the eating." You can brag about what kind of cook you are. That means nothing. Just let me eat some of your cooking. Then I will know for myself what kind of cook you are. So it is with Bible translations. You don't have to know church history. You don't have to be a Greek or Hebrew scholar or a textual scholar. Some basic facts are what you need to know. You can read and study the different English versions, compare them and you can see for yourself which is the best translation. The question is, who has produced the best translation?

Proponents of the King James Only movement use a ploy much like that of the evolutionist. By carrying you back in time billions of years, the evolutionist boggles your mind. Then they begin telling you what happened. But the human mind cannot think in terms of billions, so your mind is over-loaded and you are more receptive to their damnable error. The KJV Only writers do the same type of thing. They take the reader into discussions about things the average preacher and the everyday Christian knows little about. Then, when his mind is boggled down, they pump him full of error. I will show you things you can see and understand. I will speak in clear simple English. Let the reader judge for himself.

Suppose someone had only heard negative things about you? Suppose someone had told them only lies and slander about you and never mentioned your good points? What would they think about you? Of course, they would dislike you and maybe even hate you, although they had never met you. That is the same opinion that many people have of the NIV and NASB. You have only heard lies and slander about them. Please take another look with me.

In this book I compare the NASB and the NIV to the KJV. I think they are probably the best of the modern translations. I do not think all translations are the same. The one-man translations are not always reliable. I do not recommend the cult translations.

WERE THE KING JAMES TRANSLATORS KJV ONLY?

There is a group today that is called the King James Only. This is because they insist that the King James Version is the preserved Word of God and the only Bible for the English speaking people. They usually attack all other versions and delight in pointing out the errors in them.

I want to raise and answer the question, is this the position of the King James translators? If I can prove that the King James translators disagreed with the King James Only group in every point, then the KJV Only group does not have a leg to stand on. They base everything on the King James translators. The KJV advocates revere and lift them to the high heavens. They were superior translators, they say. You can see how inconsistent it is to be KJV Only and believe the opposite of what the KJV translators themselves believed.

In the original 1611 KJV there are eleven pages in the front called, THE TRANSLATORS TO THE READER. (See appendix A) In this introduction, the translators explained their philosophy and beliefs about Bible translations. I want to use their introduction, taking the translator's own words and show you that they disagreed with the KJV Only group in every point. In the remainder of this chapter, when a page number is given, it refers to the place where the quote can be found in THE TRANSLATORS TO THE READER, included in the back of this book. (Note: The old English has been updated for readability.)

CHAPTER 1

THEY BELIEVED THE AUTHORITY WAS IN THE ORIGINALS

On page 3 of THE TRANSLATORS TO THE READER, the King James translators said, "The original there being from heaven, not from the earth, the author's being God, not man, the editor, the Holy Spirit, not the wit of the apostles." Also on the bottom of page 9 and on the top of page 10 they said that all truth must be tried by the original tongues, the Hebrew and Greek. So the King James translators said the authority was in the originals. This is what Christians have believed throughout Church history.

On the other hand, the KJV Only group says, "No one has the originals. Have you ever seen the originals? No. You must trust the King James translation as the final authority." This assertion contradicts the KJV translators.

I do not have the original ten dollar bill but I will take all the copies you will give me. I have never seen the original constitution of the United States but thank God I have all the benefits of it. So we do not have the original copy the apostles wrote but we have around 5,000 copies of it and every word of God has been preserved in them. We do not have the original manuscripts but we do have the *original words*. We do not need the original copy, the first copy. If we had it some people would make an idol of it, I'm sure. By the way, no one has the original copy (the first manuscript) of the 1611 KJV, though many copies of the first printing exist.

The point is, the KJV translators believed the final authority was in the original Hebrew and Greek, not in any translation, including their own.

5

"The original being from Heaven...The author being God, not men."

THEY BELIEVED TRANSLATORS WERE NOT INSPIRED

On page 4 the KJV translators said the Septuagint translators were interpreters. They were not prophets. They did many things as learned men but yet as men they stumbled and fell. So the King James translators believed that translation was a purely human work. They made mistakes.

THEY DID NOT BELIEVE IN CONDEMNING OTHER VERSIONS

On page 6 the King James Translators refer to all the other English versions they had in that day. They say, "Do we condemn the ancient?... We are so far from condemning any of their labors, that translated before us, either in this land or beyond the sea. We acknowledge them to have been raised up of God for the building and furnishing of His church." So the King James translators did not believe in condemning other translations. We dare not condemn any translation, they say, unlike many people today.

The Wycliff English Bible came out in 1382. The Tyndale Bible in 1525, the Coverdale in 1535, the Rogers Bible in 1537, the Great Bible in 1539, the Geneva in 1560 and the Bishops in 1568. So when the King James Bible came out in 1611 there were many English translations just as there are today. But the King James translators did not condemn any. They did not consider other versions to be a curse but said "they had been raised up by God for the furnishing of His church." They did not believe in pointing out errors and belittling other versions of the Bible. This applied to English Translations and "those beyond the sea." They would be totally against attacking other translations like many people are doing today.

THEY BELIEVED ALL TRANSLATIONS WERE THE WORD OF GOD

On page 7, the King James translators say, "Nay, we affirm and avow that the meanest translation of the Bible in English is the word of God." When they say "meanest" they mean the poorest, the worst. So they believed that every translation was the word of God, no matter how many mistakes it had. This is the exact opposite of those who believe the King James is the only Bible for the English speaking people. Those who revere the King James translators so much believe just the opposite of what the translators themselves believed.

The translators gave several illustrations to make their point. They said the king's speech translated into another language is still the king's speech. A person can be a good person and yet have some imperfections. Someone can be a nice looking person and yet have warts or freckles, they said. And so, likewise, a translation of the Bible may have mistakes but it is still the word of God. They never said that God had promised us a perfect translation in English.

This is a very serious point. Because if the poorest translation is the word of God, then if we attack it we are attacking God's Word. Many people are doing this today. They are blaspheming God's Word. The King James translators would not belittle and attack the NIV or the NASB as many people do. They had more sense.

Dear reader, be careful how you attack other versions. The King James translators believed you are attacking the Word of God. Do not blaspheme God's Word or support those who do.

JESUS AND THE APOSTLES DID NOT ATTACK BAD TRANSLATIONS

On page 7 the King James translators said that the Septuagint, or the Seventy, "was faulty in many places. It descended from the original and did not come near it in grandeur or majesty." In other words, the Greek translation which Jesus and the apostles used was not a good translation but they did not try to tear down people's confidence in it. "Yet which of the apostles did condemn it? Condemn it! Nay! They used it." (page 7 & 8)

The point is that Jesus and the apostles had a faulty translation but they never put it down. They used it and quoted from it. They did not go around tearing down bad translations as some people do today.

Do not blaspheme and attack God's Word just because the translators made some mistakes. Jesus and the apostles did not believe in attacking other translations. The King James translators did not believe in doing that either.

THEY BELIEVED IN MAKING NEW TRANSLATIONS OFTEN

On page 8 the King James translators talk about making new translations. They ask, "Who would have ever thought that was a fault? To amend it where he saw cause?" Then they say, "That is our business. The difference that appears between our translation and our often correcting of them is the thing that we are especially charged with." It is the translator's business to continually update the language, not because God's Word is outdated, but because English changes. The English language has changed some in my lifetime. Young people do not use the same expressions as when I was a teenager. In the book, THE KING JAMES BIBLE WORD BOOK, by Ronald Bridges and Luther Weigle, the authors list 827 words that are obsolete or archaic.

Translators are not supposed to make one translation and go into retirement. It is their business to make new translations and keep them updated. That is the reason the King James translators immediately started to revise the 1611 edition and came out with another in 1613 and another in 1629 (when they left out the Apocrypha).

After reading what the KJV translators have said, I feel sure they would favor the New King James Version over the 1769 version that we use today. They said the Bible should be in the common vernacular of the people. (Page 11)

By the way, the King James Version is a British translation, not an American translation. There are a few English words that have a different meaning from ours. For example, if you go into a restaurant in England and ask for a napkin, they will give you a baby diaper.

THEY WERE NOT INSPIRED THEY SIMPLY REVISED

The KJV translators said on page 9, "Truly, good Christian reader, we never thought from the beginning that we should needs to make a new translation, or yet to make a bad one, a good one. But to make good ones better or out of many good ones, one principal good one." In other words, they said that the translations that England already had by William Tyndale, Coverdale and others were good translations. Their purpose was never to make a new translation, they said. Their purpose was to build on the labors and works of others and try to improve them. The KJV translators said the others were good translations and they tried to make them better so England could have a common Bible. They certainly succeeded in that. Thank God for the way the King James Bible has been used in so many wonderful ways. But remember, the translators did not set out to make a new inspired version. All they did was revise and update. They took the Tyndale, Cloverdale, Geneva Bible, the Pilgrim Bible and the Bishops Bible, and updated them to make a composite Bible called the 1611 King James version. That was their purpose all along. Some people think they were inspired to make a perfect translation which would be "God's preserved word for the English speaking people." This belief contradicts the King James translators. Their purpose was "to make good ones better or to make one principle good one."

There is no hint the translators thought they were inspired or anything but human translators trying to do their best. They said, "Neither did we think much to consult the Translators or Commentators...neither did we disdain to revise that which we had done, and to bring back to the anvil that which we had hammered?" (page 10)

THEY BELIEVED IN PUTTING VARYING READINGS IN THE MARGIN

On page 10 we read, "Some peradventure would have no variety of senses to be set in the margin, lest the authority of the Scripture for deciding of controversies by that show of uncertainty, should somewhat be shaken. But we hold their judgment not to be so sound in this point."

Critics object to the marginal readings in modern versions. The KJV translators included them in the 1611 version and in the TO THE READER section that we are considering now. They said a person's judgment was not sound on this point if they disagreed.

THEY DID NOT BELIEVE VARYING TRANSLATIONS EFFECTED DOCTRINE

The KJV translators said on page 10, "It hath pleased God in his divine providence, here and there to scatter words and sentences of that difficulty and doubtfulness, not in doctrinal points that concern salvation, (for in such it hath been vouched that the Scriptures are plain) but in matters of less moment."

Because every Bible doctrine is mentioned over and over, it is not possible for a mistranslation in one place to change the teaching of Scripture. No Bible doctrine is dependent on one passage. For example, the Second Coming of Christ is mentioned in over 300 places. If a passage or two were incorrectly translated or left out, still the Bible is clear, Jesus is coming again.

The KJV translators understood this truth and said the various readings did not effect "doctrinal points but in matters of less moment."

THEY SAID A VARIETY OF TRANSLATIONS WERE NECESSARY

Many People today are "King James Only." The KJV translators certainly were not. They said on page 10 that a "Variety of translations is profitable for the finding out of the sense of the Scriptures...must needs do good, yea, is necessary, as we are persuaded."

There you have it from the KJV translators themselves. They believed in using other translations. They "do good." They are "necessary."

Certainly other translations have helped me to understand many passages in God's word. Using other versions is one of the best study helps there is. KJV advocates would deprive God's people of this help.

THEY BELIEVED SCRIPTURE SHOULD BE IN COMMON LANGUAGE

Many people today think the Bible should be in old, out dated English. They object to a Bible that reads like a newspaper, in modern English.

I hate to burst your bubble but the KJV translators believed the Bible should be in modern English. The 1611 KJV was in the most up to date English when it came out.

The KJV translators said on page 11, "But we desire that the Scripture may speak like itself, as in the language, that it may be understood even of the very vulgar." They had just said how they avoided language that "darken the sense." The translators were clear, they wanted to put the scripture in the vernacular of the person on the street. They wanted the language to be so simple and up to date it could be understood by "even the very vulgar" (common, simple or uneducated). They would certainly be supportive of the modern English versions today.

CONCLUSION

What a shame today that so many exalt the KJV translators to lofty heights and yet contradict everything they stood for when it comes to Bible translations. What inconsistency!

Review what these wise men said. It is the same thing Christians have believed down through the centuries. You would be wise to stand with them and not with the modern fanatics who go contrary to the very translators they depend upon so much.

IS THE KING JAMES VERSION OF THE BIBLE INFALLIBLE?
II Peter 1:15 – 21

(In this book KJV means the King James Version. NASB means the New American Standard Bible. NIV stands for the New International Version.)

- Many people today say the KJV is the perfectly preserved Word of God in English and is the only Bible for us today.

- If I can show the KJV has many mistakes, statements that do not make sense, and verses that slander God, then obviously it is not perfect.

- Please understand that I am not attacking the Word of God, I am pointing out errors in a translation. God's Word is perfect but translations are not. God inspired the apostles and prophets when they wrote, but there is not one verse in the Bible that says translations are inspired.

- The things I point out will help you better understand your KJV. It is a very accurate translation in most places. However, it has a few places where the reader will need help to find out what God actually said.

1. In Hebrews 9:26 the KJV says, "But now once in the end of the world hath he appeared to put away sin by the sacrifice of himself." The end of the world has not come, yet Christ has already ap-

peared. Therefore this is a false statement. The New American Standard Bible (NASB) says "but now once at the consummation of the ages He has been manifested." It was at the end of the Old Testament ages that Christ appeared, not at the end of the world. The KJV mistranslates this Greek word *aion* as world. The word means age. The KJV does this about 40 times. Each time is a mistake and misleads the reader.

2. The KJV calls the Holy Spirit an "it" in Romans 8:16, 26. The NASB corrects this error and says the "Spirit Himself." The context of the whole Bible shows the Holy Spirit is not an "it." Can you, dear reader, feel comfortable calling the third person of the Trinity an "it"?

3. The KJV calls the Holy Spirit, "the Holy Ghost." The Bible says, "God is a Spirit." (John 4:24). Sometimes the KJV translates the same word as Ghost and sometimes Spirit. About 70 times they call the Holy Spirit a "Ghost" and about 250 times they translated it as "Spirit." An example is Acts 5:3,9. In verse 3 we read "Ghost" and in verse 9 we read "Spirit." It is the same word in the Greek. The NASB always translates the word as "Spirit." God is a Spirit, not a Ghost.

4. Acts 12:4 in the KJV says Herod was planning "after Easter" to bring Peter out. The KJV translates this same Greek word as "Passover" 28 times. This is the only time they translate this Greek word as "Easter." Either the translators were wrong 28 times or they are wrong in Acts 12:4. The NASB translates this Greek word as Passover all 29 times.

5. In James 5:11 the KJV says, "The Lord is very pitiful." This term is old English for God is full of pity. But still today the KJV says the Lord is "very pitiful." This is a slander against God which should be updated. The NASB says, "The Lord is full of compassion."

6. Philippians 4:6 in the KJV says, "Be careful for nothing." In every day English today this verse says "be careless about everything." The NASB correctly translates it, "Be anxious for nothing."

7. Philippians 3:20 in the KJV says, "Our conversation is in heaven." Obviously we are not talking to one another in Heaven. We are still on the earth. The NASB correctly says, "Our citizenship is in heaven."

8. In II Thessalonians 2:7 the KJV says, "Only he who now letteth will let." This is speaking of the Holy Spirit who hinders the forces of sin. The English word "let" once meant "to restrain" but today it has completely reversed in meaning. The NASB says, "He who now restrains will do so." This gives the meaning of what God actually said.

9. In modern English the word "meat" means the flesh of animals. In the KJV it means anything to eat. A "meat" offering is described in Leviticus chapter 2 but the contents contain no meat at all. In Leviticus 14:10 the KJV says, "Fine flour for a meat offering." The NASB calls it a grain offering. Many times the KJV uses the word "meat" to refer to food that has no meat in it whatsoever.

10. The word "corn" is used in the KJV 101 times. It never once means corn, as we know it today. It refers to any kind of grain. Genesis 42:1-3,5; Matthew 12:1 are examples. Remember it was the American Indians who gave us corn or "maize." The white man knew nothing about corn until after the discovery of America. Therefore, the original Bible writers could not have been referring to "corn" but rather to "grain."

11. Revelation 22:14 teaches salvation by works in the KJV. It says, "Blessed are they that do his commandments, that they may have right to the tree of life." This is a verse taken from the Latin Vulgate and inserted by Erasmus because he did not have a complete Greek manuscript of the book of Revelation. The KJV translators continued this error. There is no Greek manuscript in existence that has the KJV reading. The NASB says, "Blessed are they who have washed their robes, that they may have right to the tree of life."

12. The KJV says, "The love of money is the root of all evil," (I Timothy 6:10). This statement is certainly false. Adam and Eve did not sin for the love of money. Satan's fall was because of pride, not love of money. The adulterer and the fornicator do not do it for money, neither does the rapist. What God actually said was that money can be a root of all sorts of evil. People will do any kind of sin for money. The NASB says, "The love of money is a root of all sorts of evil."

13. In Acts 5:30 the KJV says, "The God of our fathers raised up Jesus, whom ye slew and hanged on a tree." This verse says that they killed Jesus

and then hung his corpse on a tree. Of course this contradicts all of the Gospel accounts. The NASB says, "Whom you put to death by hanging on a tree." It is easy to see which is right. The KJV makes the same mistake again in Acts 10:39, "Slew and hung on a tree."

14. In James 3:2, the KJV says we offend everybody. "In many things we offend all." The NASB says, "For we all stumble in many ways." I can agree with the NASB but not with the KJV.

15. In Acts 9:7 when Paul was converted, it says in the KJV the men "stood speechless hearing a voice, but seeing no man." In Acts 22:9 it says, "They heard not the voice of him that spake with me." Of course these verses make the Bible contradict itself. The NASB says, "Did not understand the voice of the one who spoke with me." The actual meaning of these verses is that the men heard but did not understand. The KJV makes the Bible contradict itself. The NASB does not.

16. In Acts 19:2 the KJV says, "Have ye received the Holy Ghost since ye believed?" Much false doctrine has been built on this verse. The NASB says, "Did you receive the Holy Spirit when you believed?" This translation is more accurate. It is more in line with the other Scripture teaching. The Bible clearly teaches you receive the Holy Spirit when you believe, not at some subsequent time. Ephesians 1:13 tells us, "having believed you were sealed."

17. In Song of Solomon 2:12 the KJV says, the "turtle" was singing. The NASB says the "turtle-

dove." We all know that turtles do not sing but turtledoves do.

18. The KJV uses the word "charity" for love. This is confusing because charity today means giving to the poor or needy. In I Corinthians 13:3 the KJV says, "And though I bestow all my goods to feed the poor, and though I give my body to be burned, and have not charity." Actually giving to the poor *is* charity, so the statement is a paradox. The NASB uses the word love, which makes more sense.

19. The KJV uses the word conversation about 20 times, but it never means "people talking to one another" as we use the word today. I Peter 3:1-2 is a good example of the confusion this brings to the modern reader. Here the Bible is telling the wife with an unsaved husband not to talk to win her husband but to win him by her actions, her spirit and her obedience. However, the KJV tells her to win him by her conversation; just the opposite of what God actually said. The NASB says the wife is to win the unsaved husband with her "behavior."

20. In Genesis 8:1 the KJV, speaking of the flood waters of Noah, says the "waters asswaged." I do not believe you will find this word in any dictionary. The NASB says, "the waters subsided." I can understand the NASB but I am not sure about the KJV.

CONCLUSION

The KJV is a good translation. It is accurate in most places, but if you know about the mistransla- tions and obsolete words, it will help you to understand what God actually said in the Hebrew and Greek.

There is no valid reason to reject the other good English translations we have today. In many places they can be a great help.

IS THE KING JAMES VERSION
INFALLIBLE?
Part 2

- Many people say the KJV is the preserved word of God in English. They believe it is without error. Christians have always believed it was the original Bible writers who were inspired, not the translators. It was the original writings that were perfect. The KJV translators believed this.

- There is no verse in the Bible that teaches translators are inspired. The KJV translators disclaimed inspiration for themselves.

- I want to point out some contradictions, mistakes and obsolete words in the KJV. Of course, if I can do that, it shows clearly the KJV is not infallible but it has some errors, like all other translations.

- I want to show that the NIV and NASB correct all these mistakes. Therefore other translations can be useful sometimes.

- Please understand I am not attacking the KJV. The things I point out will help you understand your KJV better. I am not saying that the KJV is inferior or that the NIV is superior. I am simply saying that it is silly to claim perfection for the KJV.

1. In the KJV it says in I Kings 4:26 that Solomon had forty thousand stalls of horses and in II Chronicles 9:25 it says he had four thousand.

These verses are an obvious contradiction. The NIV says four thousand in both places. Who would say the KJV is superior here?

2. In the KJV it says in II Kings 8:26 that Ahaziah was twenty-two years old when he began to reign. In II Chronicles 22:2 it says he was forty-two years old when he began to reign. Of course, this is a contradiction. The NIV says he was twenty-two years old in both places. Everybody knows this is better.

3. In the KJV it says in I John 3:9, "Whosoever is born of God doth not commit sin." This contradicts plain scriptures in many places. Ecclesiastes 7:20 says, "There is not a just man upon earth that doeth good and sinneth not." The NASB says in I John 3:9, "No one who is born of God practices sin." This translation is more in harmony with other scripture and with Christian experience. We sin but we do not practice sin. Our life is not characterized by sin.

4. In Exodus 25:31-38 the KJV describes the making of the candlestick for the tabernacle, but no candles are mentioned in this passage. Verse 37 says, "make the lamps thereof." The description that is given to us is a lampstand with seven branches. A beautifully wrought stand for seven lamps. The oil which the lamp would burn is described in Exodus 27:20. Throughout the KJV, the translators call a lampstand a candlestick. Examples in the New Testament where "candle-stick" should be "lampstand" are Matthew 5:15 and

Revelation 1:20, 13. The NASB always says lampstand. Certainly this is clearer.

5. In the KJV the word "quick" never means "fast." It means living or alive. In Hebrews 4:12 it says the word of God is "quick and powerful." The NASB says it is "living." The KJV says Christ will judge the "quick and the dead." (II Timothy 4:1) The NASB says the "living and the dead." It is easy to see which is more accurate.

6. In the KJV the word "prevent" is used 15 times in the Old Testament and twice in the New. Today the word "prevent" means to hinder or to stop. The Psalmist said in Psalm 119:147, "I prevented the dawning of the morning." He does not mean he hindered the dawning. The NASB says, "I rise before dawn." In I Thessalonians 4:15, the KJV says when Jesus comes the living will not "prevent" them which are asleep. The NIV says they shall not "precede" them. The Bible teaching here is that the living Christians and those who are asleep will go up together. Seventeen times the KJV obscures the meaning of the scripture by using the word "prevent." In all these cases the NASB or the NIV is much clearer.

7. In Matthew 19:9 and 5:32 the KJV gives "fornica-tion" as the only grounds for divorce under the law. Today this word means premarital sex. These verses in the KJV say the only grounds for divorce is something you did before you married. This translation grossly confuses the Bible teaching about divorce. The Greek word used here is "porneia." Both STRONG'S CONCORDANCE and

VINE'S word studies say the word is not confined to illicit sex between the unmarried but it covers all kinds of sexual immorality. It means harlotry, adultery, incest or idolatry. The NIV translates the word as "marital unfaithfulness." The NASB says "unchasity" or "immorality." Certainly this makes more sense.

8. In the KJV the word "nephew" actually means "grandson." The Hebrew word means "sons of sons." In Judges 12:14 the "thirty nephews" are changed to "thirty grandsons" in the NASB. The word "nephews" in I Timothy 5:4 in the KJV means grandchildren in the Greek. The NIV says "grand-children." The KJV can bring confusion here because it is telling us who is responsible to take care of the destitute widows in our family. The KJV says children and nephews are responsible. The NIV says children and grandchildren are to do it. It is easy to see which is right.

9. In the KJV Paul says, "I know nothing by myself." (I Cor. 4:4) The NASB says "against myself." This translation agrees with the Greek and with the context where Paul is defending himself against the accusations of the Corinthians. He is telling them that they may accuse him but his conscience is clear.

10. In the KJV Paul says, "Let your moderation be known to all men." (Phil. 4:5) People use this verse to justify mediocrity and use it to justify moderate drinking of alcoholic beverage. "Moderation" in the Greek means "gentle, kind, forbearing." The NASB says, "Let your forbearing spirit be known to all

men." The NIV says, "Let your gentleness be evident to all." Either of these is closer to the true meaning than the KJV.

11. The word "naughty" as used in the KJV can be misleading. The Hebrew and Greek words mean "very wicked." To us "naughty" means something trivial that a child or an adult might do. For example, "You naughty boy." In the KJV Jeremiah 24:2 says the figs were "so naughty" they could not be eaten. This shows the true meaning of the word by the context. The NASB says they were "very bad." The NIV and the NASB always use a better word than "naughty".

12. Many people complain that the new versions leave out things that are in the KJV. The question is not whether something is in the KJV or some other version, but rather is it in the original Hebrew and Greek? Below are some examples of phrases and words that are left out of the KJV but are in the NIV.

A. In Jude verse 25, the NIV says that God gets glory "through Jesus Christ our Lord." The KJV leaves this phrase out.
B. In Acts 4:25, the KJV says that God spoke through the mouth of David. The NIV says that God "spoke by the Holy Spirit through the mouth of David." The KJV leaves out the "Holy Spirit."
C. In Acts 16:7 the KJV says, "the Spirit suffered them not." The NIV says, "the Spirit of Jesus would not allow them to." "Of Jesus" is left out of the KJV.

D. In Philippians 1:14, "of God" is left out of the KJV. The NIV says the "word of God." The KJV simply says "word."

E. In Colossians 2:9, the KJV says "in Him." The NIV says "in Christ."

When things are left out of the modern versions, some people claim there was a conspiracy or the translators were biased against the deity of Christ, etc. Why did the KJV leave these words and phrases out?

13. Some people say the NIV and the NASB are weak on the deity of Christ. This is a lie. I will show you some key verses on the deity of Christ and anyone can clearly see the KJV is the weakest on this subject.

A. Jude 4 in the KJV says, "denying the only Lord God and our Lord Jesus Christ." By adding an "and," the KJV makes it appear like God and the Lord Jesus are different persons. The NIV says, "deny Jesus Christ our only Sovereign and Lord." The KJV separates God and Christ. The NIV makes God and Christ one. Also, "Jesus Christ our only Sovereign and Lord" is stronger than "our Lord Jesus Christ."

B. In Titus 2:13, the KJV inserts the word "our" and makes it sound like God and Jesus are different. It says, "The great God and our Saviour Jesus Christ." The NIV and NASB both say, "Our great God and Saviour Jesus Christ." They make it clear that the great God is the same as the Saviour Jesus Christ. Three times in Titus the expression, "God our Saviour" is used. (Titus 1:3; 2:10; 3:4) In Titus 2:13 when he finally reveals who the "God and Saviour" is, the KJV obscures it. This mistake effects at least four verses about the Deity of Christ.

C. The KJV adds "our" again in II Peter 1:1, "Righteousness of God and our Saviour Jesus Christ." The NIV says, "God and Saviour Jesus Christ." The KJV makes it appear like "God and Saviour" are two different persons. The NIV and NASB make it clear they are one and the same.

D. In Colossians 2:9 the KJV says, "For in Him dwelleth all the fullness of the Godhead bodily." The NIV says, "For in Christ all the fullness of deity lives in bodily form." The NIV is definitely clearer and stronger.

E. In Philippians 2:6 the KJV says, "Who, being in the form of God." The NIV says, "Who, being in the very nature of God." The "very nature of God" is certainly better than "the form of God."

F. In Romans 9:5 the KJV says, "of whom as concerning the flesh Christ came, who is over all, God blessed forever." The NIV says, "from them is traced the human ancestry of Christ, who is God over all, forever praised." It is hard to see the deity of Christ in the KJV but it is crystal clear in the NIV.

G. In John 1:18 the KJV says, "No man hath seen God at any time; the only begotten son, which is in the bosom of the Father, He hath declared

Him." The NIV says, "No man has ever seen God, but God the one and only, who is at the Father's side, has made Him known." Certainly "God the one and only" is stronger and better than "only begotten Son." All Christians are "begotten" by God. (I John 5:1,18.) Christ alone is "God the one and only."

These examples were given to show anyone who is willing to see that the NIV is stronger than the KJV on the deity of Christ in many places. The KJV obscures the deity of Christ in some places. The NIV reinforces the teaching of the deity of Christ. There have been many lies told about this subject but now you know.

14. The KJV sometimes uses the word "charity" in the place of love. Most people probably think charity is old English for "love." That is not the case. William Tyndale, who translated the first English version in 1525, used only the word "love." So did the other versions that followed (Coverdale, Matthew, Great Bible and Geneva Bible). Only the second edition of the Bishops Bible and the KJV use the word "charity". The noun "agape" is used 114 times in the Greek. The KJV translates it "love" 87 times and "charity" 26 times. This shows they knew the Greek word means "love." Yet they purposely translated the word as "charity" in some places. "Charity" means giving and helping the needy. Love is described in I Corinthians 13. The KJV weakens this basic Christian doctrine about God and man by substituting "charity" for "love." They did it in about 18 other places. The modern

versions undergird it by rightly translating agape as love.

Conclusion

Anyone who is not willingly ignorant and blind can see that the King James Version is not perfect and not infallible. It is a human translation. It is a good and accurate version in most places. But sometimes you will need the good modern translations. Other translations can really help you understand what God actually said in some verses. Don't let anyone deprive you of this help.

Please understand that I am not putting down the KJV. I am not saying it is inferior or that the NIV is superior. I am saying the KJV is not perfect. The NIV and the NASB can help you sometimes. The KJV translators themselves said, "A variety of translations is profitable for the finding out of the sense of the Scriptures...must needs do good, yea, is necessary, as we are persuaded." (TO THE READER section, 1611 KJV)

Don't let anyone lie to you saying the KJV is God's perfectly preserved word without error, and don't listen to the slander against the NIV and the NASB.

Again let me say, I am not against the KJV. I am against the KJV Only extremism.

CHAPTER 4

WERE THE EARLY FUNDAMENTALISTS KJV ONLY?
or
What is the historic Christian position on Bible translations?

Of all the hundreds of Bible translations around the world today and in different generations past, some people select the King James Version as the only one they use or recognize. They claim the King James translation is inspired just as the original writings were. This is certainly a claim the translators never made for themselves! The Bible says inspiration stopped when Revelation chapter 22 was complete. (Rev. 22:18-19)

Some KJV Only people disclaim inspiration for the KJV translators but they say the KJV is God's perfectly preserved Word. That is the same thing as inspiration. It takes inspiration to have perfection.

I know some will scream at this point and say they believe in perfect preservation, not inspiration for the KJV. That is playing with words. It is not being completely honest. The bottom line is, if something is perfect, it has to be inspired. Call it what you will. To claim perfection for the KJV is to claim inspiration.

Inspiration in the Bible refers only to the original manuscripts. Each translation has to be judged on its own merits, or lack of them. This includes the KJV which is really only a revised version itself, being based on William Tyndale's translation and the Bishops Bible.

HISTORIC FUNDAMENTAL POSITION

The historic fundamental position has always been that inspiration is claimed only for the original Greek and Hebrew manuscripts. Dr. Robert L. Sumner, in his booklet on BIBLE TRANSLATIONS quotes all the great men of the past who were known to be leaders in Fundamental circles. He also quotes the greatest leaders living at the time he wrote, and all of them agree that the historic Christian position has always been that inspiration concerns the original writings and each translation has to be evaluated individually. Listed below are some of these leaders and what they have said concerning Bible translations and versions. The next eight paragraphs are quotes from BIBLE TRANSLATIONS by Dr. Robert L. Sumner.

1. Dr. George S. Bishop said, "We take the ground that on the original parchment -the membrane-every sentence, word, line, mark, point, pen-stroke, jot, tittle was put there by God. On the original parchment." (page 12)

2. Dr. William Bell Riley said that people make sort of a fetish of the King James Version. "To claim, therefore, inerrancy for the King James Version, or even for the Revised Version, is to claim inerrancy for men who never professed it for themselves." He says further,... "The accepted versions of the Bible are all substantially correct." (page 13)

3. R. A. Torrey said, "By the Bible I do not mean any particular English version of the Scriptures - the Authorized Version, the Revised, or any other version - but the Scriptures as originally given. Furthermore, all versions are a substantially

accurate rendition of the Hebrew and Aramaic..." (page 14)

4. Charles H. Spurgeon quoted and argued from many versions including the Catholic, Syriac, and the English Revised Version. He pointed out wrong translations in the King James Version. Spurgeon said, "Do not needlessly amend our Authorized Version. It is faulty in many places, but still is a grand work taking it for all in all... Correct where correction must be for truth's sake..." (page 16)

5. Dr. G. Campbell Morgan said, "You ask me which is the best translation of the New Testament. I do not hesitate to say that it is the American Revision." (page 16)

6. Dr. John R. Rice said, "The beauty, the stately dignity and reverence of the language is far beyond that of any other translation." This is what he said about the King James Version, but referring to inspiration he said, "When we say that the Bible is inspired, we do not refer to the translations or copies but to the original autographs." "Translations are not inspired," he said. (page 17)

7. Dr. C. I. Scofield, when asked about which Bible to use for public work, said, "The King James, or Authorized Version, remains the Bible of the people, and is, therefore, best for the minister's public work. He should, of course, be acquainted with the revised renderings of all the passages in which important changes are made, and should not hesitate to call attention to the better and clearer readings." (page 19)

8. Dr. Robert Sumner quotes many other writers to show that *all* the fundamental leaders have always believed that the Bible was inspired in it's original writings. No translation should be considered inspired or "God breathed" like the Greek and Hebrew was. Others quoted by Dr. Sumner in his booklet include Dr. Louis T. Talbot, Dr. William Graham Scroggie, Dr. Arthur T. Pierson, Dr. B. H. Carroll, Dr. John A. Broadus, Dr. Carl McIntire, Dr. Richard V. Clearwaters and Dr. James M. Gray, etc.

9. On page 1213 in the Old Scofield Bible, the note at the bottom of the page says, "The writers of scripture invariably affirm, where the subject is mentioned by them at all, that the words of their writings are divinely taught. This, of necessity, refers to the <u>original documents, not to translations</u> and versions; but the labours of competent scholars have brought our English version<u>s</u> to a degree of perfection so remarkable that we may confidently rest upon <u>them</u> as authoritative." (underlines added)

The list of eight consulting editors at the front of the Scofield Bible reads like a "Who's Who" in the world of Bible believing scholars in the early 1900's. This group of Bible college presidents, authors, teachers, and editors all agreed with the note quoted above. So this note becomes a powerful testimony as to what early fundamentalists believed.

WRITINGS MAKE IT CLEAR

The very people who helped to organize and to write the beliefs of what is called "Fundamentalism" today make it clear what they believed. The great recognized writings such as THE FUNDAMENTALS and THE HISTORY OF FUNDAMENTALISM IN AMERICA, make it clearly known how Bible believers have always stood. They all believed the same as stated above.

The paradox of our times is that some people say only the King James is perfect, and they who believe this are the only real Fundamentalists. All others are Pseudo, or hypocrite Fundamentalists. The fact is, the KJV Only group is a new fundamentalism. It is a new cult developed within the fundamental movement.

BIBLE BELIEVING LEADERS TODAY

Most of the Bible believing leaders of today are not KJV Only. Very few of the evangelicals are KJV Only. Most of the leading Bible schools and seminaries are not KJV Only. Examples are Bob Jones University, Tennessee Temple and Liberty University. The Baptist Bible Fellowship is the largest Independent Baptist Fellowship, and it is not KJV Only. Most of the great preachers of today are not KJV Only.

The Fundamental Baptist Fellowship said in their news bulletin for July/August, 1984 "We reject as heretical the concept that any translation of the Bible is given by inspiration, which has in our generation fostered a cult. We believe firmly that inspiration ceased upon the closure of the canon of Scripture in the original autographs. We likewise reject the practice of exalting any version or translation to the position held uniquely by the original writings."

BIBLE SCHOOLS AND SEMINARIES

It is important to notice that all reputable Bible schools which have stood for the inspiration of the Scripture, have always believed just as presented above.

Peter Ruckman originated the King James Only view. Before the 1950's there were no Christians, Bible Schools, church fathers, martyrs or scholars who restricted Christians to the use of only one version of the Bible. Peter Ruckman admits this in his book, THE ALEXANDRIAN CULT, part one: "Every recognized church historian and Christian scholar is a member of the cult. This cult is the Alexandrian Cult of North Africa, and its tentacles stretch from Origen (184-254 AD) to John R. Rice and the faculty members of every recognized school in the world." By "Alexandrian Cult" he meant those who recommend using other versions besides the King James. The King James Only view is Ruckmanism and is opposed to all Christendom now and in the past. This is a tremendous truth. I hope the reader can absorb the impact of this statement. Only those poisoned by Ruckmanism are KJV Only.

If one goes against all the great Christian scholars of the past and present, he is sure to make a fool of himself. We should not believe something just because someone else does. On the other hand, anyone who goes off after a new doctrine different from the accepted historic Christian position is bound to be wrong because we have the faith "once delivered to the saints." (Jude 3) If any doctrine is new, then it is not true. And if it is true, then it is not new.

The KJV Only view is a new doctrine to Christians. However, it is not completely new in the world of heresy, because the Roman Catholics claimed the same thing for their Latin Vulgate translation. About 16 popes pronounced the Vulgate infallible. Later Clement VIII had it revised and corrected. To claim a translation is infallible is an old Roman Catholic heresy.

TEXTUS RECEPTUS

Some of the KJV fans claim it is the only infallible version because it was translated from the "Textus Receptus." Dr. Allan A. MacRae and Dr. Robert C. Newman in their booklet entitled THE TEXTUS RECEPTUS AND THE KING JAMES VERSION, show that the "Textus Receptus" was not published until 1624, which was 13 years after the KJV. Therefore the KJV could not have been translated from it. In other words, it was not actually called the Textus Receptus until 1624.

The KJV was based on the Stephanus text, which is a revision of Erasmus' Greek text , now called the Textus Receptus. Erasmus, a Roman Catholic, prepared the Greek text that later became known as the Textus Receptus. In other words, Erasmus' Greek text evolved into what today is called the Textus Receptus. Technically speaking, the Textus Receptus was not in existence when the KJV was translated in 1611. Scholars have pointed out that the Stephanus text differs from the Textus Receptus in 287 places. In other words, the Textus Receptus is supposed to be the perfect Greek text and the KJV is supposed to be perfect because it was translated from that text. Yet the KJV was translated from a Greek text that differs from it in

287 places. How does one explain these differences?

Some people assume that the Erasmus text, the Textus Receptus, the Stephanus text and the majority text are all the same. That is not the case. Dr. Wilbur Pickering admits that the Erasmus text differed from the majority text in about a thousand places. (THE IDENTIITY OF THE NEW TESTAMENT TEST, P. 177, footnote 1) Where does this leave those who say the KJV is perfect because it was translated from a perfect "Textus Receptus"? They don't know what the Textus Receptus is.

Erasmus put some words in the Book of Revelation that are not found in any Greek manuscript whatever. That is the reason why Revelation 22:14, in the KJV, teaches works for salvation.

Much work has been done since Erasmus prepared his Greek text from a few moderately ancient manuscripts. The number of manuscripts has increased today and work has reached such perfection that no more than one word in a thousand is questioned. And even these have no bearing on any doctrine, precept or promise. Most textual scholars seem to agree on this.

CONCLUSION

The King James Version is accurate and trustworthy. It may be the best version to use for public teaching and preaching. But we may receive help from other good translations by Bible believing scholars.

One who claims the KJV is the infallible translation and all others are to be rejected as heretical, is going against the historic Fundamental stand. They are building a doctrine for which there is absolutely no Scripture to back it up. It is a completely new man-made doctrine that even King James translators themselves would not defend. One should never say, "The Bible is our sole rule for all matters of faith and practice," if they contend for the inspiration of any translation. For that is not taught anywhere in any Bible.

KJV ONLY DIVIDES THE BODY OF CHRIST

The Bible says we should all endeavor "to keep the unity of the Spirit in the bond of peace." (Eph. 4:3) But some people use the KJV to break the unity and the peace. They make the KJV the test of fellowship with other Christians. I want to get along with all God's people whether they agree with me or not. All that believe the Bible is God's Word should love one another and not make any version the test of Christian fellowship. Those who break fellowship with everyone who does not have a KJV Only view are dividing God's people. God hates those that cause a division among His people. (Proverbs 6:19)

NOT ALL TRANSLATIONS ARE THE SAME

There are some translations by liberals, modernists, and some by false cults that have serious errors and should be rejected. But even these teach the same Bible doctrines as good reliable translations. I have used Jehovah's Witnesses own Watchtower translation to prove them wrong. It is wise sometimes to use the Catholic translations when witnessing to Catholics.

Certainly all translations by good, Bible believing scholars teach the very same thing. Regardless of what version I would read and preach from, I would still believe and preach the same thing as I do now. I can take any version of the Bible and prove to anyone what I believe.

Some seem to think that if you change one word, then you destroy some major teaching. They don't understand the way the Bible is written. Every doctrine of the Bible is mentioned over and over. No doctrine is mentioned just once and then never mentioned again later on. The Bible is a progressive revelation. For example, the second coming of Christ was mentioned by Enoch (Jude 14), but it is mentioned again and again over 300 times. If a translation was faulty in one place it would not change what the Bible taught about this subject. There are still plenty of passages that do prove it.

TRUTH CANNOT BE DESTROYED BY MISTRANSLATION

God in His wisdom has written the Bible so that it cannot be destroyed by mistranslation. Bible teachings do not depend on the correct translation of some word or words. The words "substitute" and "Trinity" are not found at all in the Bible, but the teaching is certainly there. The virgin birth of Christ can be proven from long passages without using the word "virgin." The teaching about hell can be proven without using the word "hell" at all. But of course the word hell is used.

Suppose someone left out or mistranslated the word "believe" in John 3:16. Would this destroy the Bible doctrine of Salvation by faith? Of course not! We have the word "believe" used several times in this same chapter. (vs. 15, 18, 36). Suppose some version left out the whole chapter? We would have the rest of John to prove it. But suppose a version left out the entire book of John? We would still have Romans, Acts, etc. If we did not even have a New Testament we could still show "the just shall live by faith." (Hab. 2:4) The apostles and the New Testament church did not have anything except the Old Testament. They still preached salvation by faith in the Lord Jesus Christ. The point is that the Bible cannot be destroyed by mistranslation. The only way to get rid of the Bible teaching is to get rid of the whole Bible.

Let me make it clear that I do not condone the intentional mistakes and errors that some translators have made. No indeed! I am just making the point that all of it is the powerful Word of God. You do not have to have a complete copy of the Bible to make it so. Looking at history and mankind as a whole, there have been very few people comparatively, who have had a complete copy. Many Christians and some pastors in foreign lands today do not have a complete Bible. They still believe and preach the pure gospel of Christ.

One does not have to have a whole Bible, with every word perfect, to have the Bible message.

CHAPTER 5

WE CAN BE SURE OUR
TRANSLATIONS ARE ACCURATE

Some folks delight in destroying people's faith in all other translations except the KJV. Let me list some reasons below which prove we have accurate English translations.

1. Scholars can compare old Greek manuscripts and thus omit errors. For example, if two errors exist out of 1,000 manuscripts of the same text, then when they compare them all together, and they find in a certain place, two are different from the rest. They can assume the two are wrong and thus omit errors. In other words, they can compare Greek manuscripts and those few which do not agree with the vast majority can be assumed to be a copyist error.

2. You can compare translations. There are probably about 100 English translations today. They are made by different scholars and groups of scholars in different places and at different times. So when they all come up with translations that teach the same things, they must be right. All translations teach the same doctrines. There will be places or verses that will be different. In these places you can compare translations just as the manuscripts discussed above. In other words, you can compare translations, and the ones that are different from the majority, may be assumed to be wrong.

3. Each person who can read Greek can check translations to make sure they are right. There are those who are continually doing this. Our transla-

41

tions have been checked literally millions of times by these people. If there are discrepancies or doubtful translations in some verse, you can be sure scholars know about them.

4. A person can check the Bible for himself if he is interested enough to obtain a STRONG's concordance. With this book anyone who can use an English dictionary can check the meaning of any Greek word. Also, there are books on word studies which have the meaning of Greek words explained in English. VINE's word studies is a good example. Even a person who knows nothing about the original languages, can check the meaning of any Greek or Hebrew word and see if it is translated correctly. Many Christians are continually doing this.

5. God guarantees to preserve His word. By this we know we have God's word with us today. He does not promise to preserve His word perfectly in one particular translation as some people claim. The Bible does not say the KJV is God's perfectly preserved word.

God has made it possible for us to know exactly what He has said in His book. You can check out any doubtful verse for yourself if you wish.

INTERESTING FACTS

Every translation is God's word in so far as it is translated correctly. Out of the 31,124 verses in the Bible, there are only about 200 or less that are even questioned, regardless of what translation you use or what family of Greek manuscripts you use. This means there are over 30,900 verses that are God's word. So in any translation you use, the vast majority of it is the word of God. This is why the KJV translators said, "The meanest translation is the word of God."

The differences between translations has been grossly exaggerated by some. The differences between families of Greek manuscripts have also been magnified and blown out of proportion by Ruckman, Riplinger, Waite, and others. These people make a lot of money appealing to the ignorance of God's people. The fact is, both the Textus Receptus and the Alexandrian manuscripts set forth every doctrine that God has inspired. There is no important doctrinal difference. It is the same with the different English translations. Peter Ruckman said he had problems with only 152 verses of the New Testament (THE CHRISTIAN'S HANDBOOK OF MANUSCRIPT EVIDENCE, page 89).

Some people go to great extremes to magnify the differences between translations and families of Greek manuscripts. These same people go to great extremes to play down the differences in the KJV and the Textus Recptus. In II Timothy chapter two, I counted 55 changes from the 1611 KJV to the 1769 version of the KJV that we use today. If you multiply 55 by 1189, (the number of chapters in the Bible), you can see there are at least 50,000 differences between the original KJV and the one we use today. The KJV Only people scream about the differences between the KJV and the NIV but excuse the changes within the KJV. They say the differences in the five major editions of the KJV were corrections in spelling, words, etc. The changes did not effect doctrine, they say. This is also true of the changes between the KJV and the NIV. However, the KJV Only group magnify the changes in the NIV and minimize the changes in the KJV.

The same is true when it comes to Greek Manuscripts. The KJV Only crowd screams about the differences in the families of manuscripts, but say nothing about the differences in the 18 editions of the Textus Recptus. Yes, there have been 18 different editions of the Textus Recptus with no two alike (some say 30 editions). When they say the Textus Recptus are the only inspired manuscripts, which edition do they mean? Why do the differences in the other manuscripts mean so much, and the differences in the Textus Recptus mean nothing? It sounds like someone is abandoning all logic and is trying to prove a point with no facts or Scripture.

CONCLUSION

When you read the Bible, you can be sure you are reading the word of God. Since God never promised a perfect translation, you may have to occasionally check some detail in the original or compare translations. But this is the exception rather than the rule.

The believer should read his Bible searching for blessings and to see Christ, not searching for flaws. Let the textual scholars work these few problems out.

WHICH BIBLE?

Many people have written books claiming the KJV is without error. They say it is God's perfectly preserved word with no mistakes.

Peter Ruckman says over and over in his book, HANDBOOK OF MANUSCRIPT EVIDENCE, that the KJV is superior to the original Greek. He says where the Greek says one thing and the Authorized Version (A.V.) says another, " throw out the Greek." Ruckman says the A.V. 1611 is necessary to recover the original text and straighten out the corrupt Greek. "The A.V. 1611 is correct; the Greek texts are wrong." (p. 125) Again and again Ruckman says the KJV is the final authority. William Grady has written a book called THE FINAL AUTHORITY in which he says the KJV is the final authority, not the original Greek and Hebrew.

The KJV Only folks tell us the KJV had superior translators, superior manuscripts, and therefore is a superior translation. The KJV Only people tell us that translators of other Bible versions were unbelievers. They assert the other translators were biased against the deity of Christ. They allege other versions left verses out.

Have we been lied to about Bible versions? I want the reader to compare the facts and decide for himself.

SOURCES FOR OUR TRANSLATIONS

The New American Standard Bible used around 5,000 Greek manuscripts dating back to the 3rd and 4th centuries. The translators used early versions in other languages, plus writings of the early church fathers who quoted the Bible in their writings.

These three sources- manuscripts, versions, and fathers- were all combined for the first time. There were almost 100 Bible believing scholars from different denominations who translated this version.

The New International version used over 100 scholars working with the best available Hebrew, Aramaic and Greek texts. The group was transdenominational and international. There were people from the United States, Great Britain, Canada, Australia and New Zealand working together.

There were many denominations that included Anglican, Assemblies of God, Baptist, Brethren, Lutheran, Mennonite, Methodist, Nazarene, Presbyterian and others. This was to safeguard the translation from sectarian bias. No other translation has gone through a more thorough process of review and revision from committee to committee than this one. They tried to make every effort to produce an accurate contemporary English translation.

Erasmus, who compiled the Textus Receptus, from which the KJV was translated, used 6 manuscripts, none older than the 9th century. Some scholars say none were older than the 12th century. All together there was not a complete copy of the New Testament. Verses were copied out of the Roman Catholic Latin Bible to complete the book of Revelation. He had only a fraction of the copies of Greek manuscripts available today.

THE GREEK TEXT

The Greek text used by the NASB was compiled by Bible believing scholars such as Ellicott, Alford, Lightfoot, Westcott and Hort. Their Greek text was approved by the greatest Greek scholars such as A.T. Roberson and Gresham Machen.

The Greek text used by the KJV translators was compiled by Erasmus, who was a liberal Roman Catholic. He added verses from the Catholic Latin translation. It was the work of one man. There has been 18 editions of this Textus Receptus with no two exactly alike.

TRANSLATORS

The NASB was translated by about 100 of the best scholars in Europe and America. They were Baptist, Presbyterian, Methodist and other denominations to omit bias. As I have already stated, the NIV had scholars from all over the English speaking world. There were many denominations represented on the translation committee.

The KJV was translated by the Church of England (called the Episcopal Church in the U.S.). They reveal their bias by refusing to translate words like "baptism" and "deacon," because if they did, it would contradict the practice of their church. The KJV originally contained the Apocrypha, 14 books and 172 chapters of uninspired writings from the Catholic Bible. Also, it contained a list of holy days, including one for the "blessed Virgin." There was not a big variety of denominations on the KJV translation committee. There was not one Baptist. King James hated Baptists. He said he wanted to "harrow out of England" all Baptists.

King James selected 54 learned men from high churchmen and some Puritans. He tried to secure the cooperation of every Biblical scholar of note in his kingdom. The translators were instructed to use the Bishops' Bible as a basis and departed from it only when the text required it. It was to have no marginal notes, except for the explanation of Hebrew and Greek words. This last simple rule, probably more than anything else, helped to make our Authorized Version the Bible of all classes in England and America. All versions before the KJV had notes. King James did not like some of these notes. This is one reason the king wanted a new translation.

Never before had such labor and care been expended on an English Bible. The result was a translation with grace and dignity and masterful English.

TRANSLATION FINISHED

The American Standard Version came out in 1901 and has been rightly regarded for its scholarship and accuracy. It was a product of both British and American scholarship. Nearly a hundred scholars labored 10 years. In 1959 a new translation project was launched, based on the ASV. There were about 100 more eminent scholars who labored. The result was the New American Standard Bible.

The Lockman Foundation said their fourfold aim was (1) be true to the original Hebrew, Aramaic and Greek. (2) be grammatically correct (3) be understandable to the masses (4) give the Lord Jesus Christ His proper place.

The KJV, on the other hand, was finished in 1611. The translators revised it in 1613, making about 400 changes. They revised it again in 1629, leaving out the Apocrypha. It has been revised at least 5 times. The last revision was in 1769. It still has at least 400 outdated words. Some today think they still have the 1611 edition, when in fact, we have the 1769 edition. If you did have a 1611 edition, it would be very valuable, worth at least a hundred thousand dollars probably. When people today say they have a 1611 KJV, it is gross ignorance on their part.

THE RESULT

The result for the NASB and the NIV is a contemporary and easy to understand Bible in modern English. They are an accurate translation of the original Greek and Hebrew.
The result for the KJV is a good translation with beautiful old English. However, it has many outdated words and some obvious mistakes.

EXAMPLES OF OUTDATED WORDS

The KJV says in I Peter 3:8 that we are to "be pitiful." This is old English for "be full of pity." II Cor. 8:1 says, "We do you to wit of the grace of God bestowed on the churches of Macedonia." Joshua 9:5 says, "clouted upon their feet." Exodus 19:18 says, "Mount Sinai was altogether on a smoke." These verses can be hard for the modern reader to understand. With the modern translations one does not have to deal with outdated words.

NAMES ARE A PROBLEM

The KJV sometimes uses the Greek form, the Latin form or the Hebrew form of the same name. Examples of this is Joshua and Jesus used for same Old Testament character. (Acts 7:45; Heb.4:8) Different spellings are used for Cis and Kish; Noe and Noah; Kora and Core; Hosea and Osee; Isaiah

and Esay; Judas, Judah, Juda and Jude; Elijah and
Elias; Elisha and Eliseus, etc.

CONCLUSION

I believe it is misguided for fundamental Baptists
to defend a version of the Bible based on a Greek
text, prepared by a liberal Roman Catholic, translated by Episcopalians and authorized by a king
who hated Baptists. While they reject translations
based on a Greek text approved by all the great
scholars and early fundamental leaders and translated by good Bible believing scholars from all
groups, including Baptists. A.T. Robertson was the
greatest Greek scholar America ever produced. He
was a conservative Baptist and approved of the
American Standard Version. This irony is strange
indeed when fundamental Baptists take sides with
Episcopalians and Catholics and reject their own.

I also find it disturbing that the KJV Only group
can write books, preach sermons and talk continually against all other versions. However, the minute
I point out errors in the KJV, they call me a "Bible
corrector" and an unbeliever, and other names.
Why is it all right for them to blaspheme God's word
found in other versions but no one can even point
out undeniable facts about the KJV?

I want to solemnly warn those who condemn all
translations besides the KJV that they are blaspheming God's word. Those who magnify the
differences between Greek texts and versions are
blaspheming God's word. If a person wants to use
only the KJV, that is well and good. However, if
they tear down all other versions, they are destroying people's faith in God's word. That is a wicked
sin. Those who insist on a KJV Only view are

causing a division in the body of Christ. This is a very serious sin. Do not be a partaker of their evil deeds. God will hold you responsible. (Psalm 138:2; Romans 14:12) Be sure you are worshiping King Jesus and not King James.

WHY NEW VERSIONS ARE NEEDED

From Tyndale's Bible in 1525 until today, there is a history of growth and improvement by means of repeated Bible revisions. Tyndale revised his translation several times. The English versions which followed are but revisions and improvements of Tyndale's first English Bible, until we come to the Bishops' Bible in 1568. The 1611 KJV is one of the best proofs of the value of Bible revision, being a revision of the Bishops' version. The KJV has been revised about 5 times, the last in 1769, which is the one we use today.

Revisions and new translations will always be needed because language changes, and it needs to be updated. Today we have a treasury of ancient manuscripts, versions and quotations that the KJV translators never dreamed of. The science of textual criticism has improved drastically. Scholars today have a better understanding of the original languages. This kind of knowledge has accumulated considerably in the almost 400 years since 1611.

William Tyndale said in the preface of his first English New Testament that if anyone could find an inaccuracy that did not give the exact sense of the original language, he should correct it. Tyndale said, "remembering that so is their duty to do so."

Some people seem to think the KJV translators were an elect group inspired by God in a special way to produce a perfect translation. When, in fact, every Christian has as much right to translate as any other. Every Christian can check the meaning of words in the original language. It is his obligation to do so. The Bible says, "Study to show yourself approved unto God."

Remember the KJV translators criticized their own version and corrected it in many places. Then they came out with new editions, in 1613 and 1629. Some people accuse me of blasphemy when I point out errors in the KJV. I am doing the same thing the KJV translators did when they corrected their own version. Also, people condemn the NASB or the NIV for revising and correcting, just like the KJV translators did.

IMPORTANT FACTS ABOUT BIBLE TRANSLATION

1. Inspiration refers to the original writings. Over and over the prophets claimed, "The word of the Lord came unto me" or "God spoke to me saying." (Ezek. 1:3;Jere. 11:1) The apostle Paul claimed that the words he was speaking to the Corinthians were not his own but words the Spirit of God was giving him. (I Cor. 12:13) These Bible writers were claiming Divine inspiration. They were the original writers. When Revelation chapter 22 was completed, inspiration stopped. (Rev. 22:18-19) To claim inspiration for anything since is to add to the Scriptures and bring a curse upon yourself.

2. The KJV Only group is doing the same thing as the Mormons do when they add the Book of Mormon to the Scripture. They are doing the same thing the Charismatics do when they get a "new revelation" through tongues. When the KJV Only advocates claim inspiration for the KJV or say it is God's perfectly preserved word, they are doing the same thing. Asserting perfection for the KJV Bible

is the same as saying it is inspired. This is dangerous. (I have read all the explanations and arguments the KJV advocates give about the difference
between inspiration and preservation. I understand
them. I still stick with my statement above.)

3. All translations teach the same thing because no
Bible doctrine depends on one verse or the proper
translation of a word. Every Bible doctrine is
mentioned over and over. Therefore it cannot be
destroyed by mistranslation. For example: The
word "Lord" is mentioned 749 times. The word
"hell" is mentioned 51 times (plus the terms like
lake of fire, furnace of fire, eternal punishment, etc).
You can easily see that if "hell" was left out in one
place or several places, it would not change the
Bible teaching on the subject.

There is no Bible doctrine at stake regardless of
what translation you use or which family of manuscripts you use. In other words, any Bible doctrine
you mention is in all translations. Every Bible
doctrine is in the Textus Receptus manuscripts.
They are also in the Alexandrian manuscripts. There
are some differences, but all doctrines are in both
families of manuscripts. A doctrine may be ad-
versely affected in a certain passage of a particular
translation, but it is still mentioned over and over in
all families of manuscripts.

4. Today, even though we do not possess the
original manuscripts and even though there are
variant readings, we can be sure we have the word
of God. Because the copies taken together, give us
100 percent of the original manuscripts. This
means nothing has been lost that God inspired.

There is less than 2% variation between the 5,300 Greek manuscripts that we have today. Textual scholars tell us that even the manuscripts that vary the most would not effect fundamentally the message of the Scriptures. In the small area where word differences among copies do exist, textual scholars attempt to determine the most probable original reading. This way they can establish the original text close to 99% of the time. This means that all translators are translating the same Greek text about 99% of the time.

A. T. Robertson was probably the greatest American Greek Scholar ever. He was familiar with the most minute details of the Greek text. He said the textual variants amounted to only "a thousandth part of the entire text." Westcott and Hort estimated the New Testament text was 98.33% pure whether or not one used the TEXTUS RECEPTUS or their own Greek text. Philip Schaff estimated there were only 400 variants that affected the sense of a passage, and only 50 were actually important and none affected any article of faith or Christian duty. Most scholars believe that 90% of the varying readings have been resolved. So this leaves only 10% of 1%, not enough to be greatly concerned about.

B. B. Warfield said, "the great bulk of the New Testament has been transmitted to us without, or almost without, any variations. It can be asserted with confidence that the sacred text is exact and valid and that no article of faith and no moral precept in it has been distorted or lost." The great Old Testament scholar Dr. Robert Dick Wilson said, "I can affirm that there is not a page of the Old Testament concerning which we need have any doubt."

All this means that Christians can trust their Bibles today. Since the extant copies of manuscripts can be shown to be 99% like the original and the remaining inconsequential 1% still contains the original among the variants, then there is no reason to doubt that we have the same inerrant Word of God that the prophets and apostles delivered to us.

John Ankerberg commented about all the exaggerated concern the KJV Only groups show over the 1% of the text, when this one percent does not deal in important matters, is like risking your life to save a million dollars which is safely in the bank.

LET US BE THANKFUL

We are blessed to have the Word of God today. In most places in the world, the Bible is hard to get. Throughout history the vast majority of people have not had a complete Bible. Noah and Abraham did not have a Bible. Moses and Israel only had the first few books. David had less than half of the Old Testament. The early Christians and Paul had only the Old Testament. In the first few centuries of Christianity, there were few copies of the Bible. Not until the invention of the printing press did the Bible become affordable and widespread. Many times governments have outlawed and persecuted people for possessing a copy of the Word of God.

We should be thanking and praising God for all the Bibles we have today, for the KJV and the other reliable versions. We are rich. We are blessed. We should be on our faces worshipping, instead of being in each others faces bickering over the relatively minor differences in translations.

HAVE WE BEEN LIED TO?

In this chapter I will show the KJV Only group has repeatedly lied and misrepresented the facts, not just a few times, but over and over. This is the way they propagate their theory. Lying and deception is normal for them.

NEW AGE VERSIONS

Gail Riplinger's writings are a good example of distortion, twisting the facts and outright lying. When I was sent an advertisement of her NEW AGE VERSIONS, it was evident this book was extreme and way out in left field. She claimed there was a hidden alliance between the new Bible versions and the New Age Movement. She asserted that the New Versions had occult origins. They would prepare the churches of the last day to accept the religion of the Anti-Christ and to receive his mark.

Anyone in his right mind knows that no Bible will do this. The New Age movement is not built on any Bible. The Anti-Christ will not have any kind of Bible. He will be against all Bibles. Later on I learned that many gullible people were buying Riplinger's book. That is unbelievable, I thought.

When I saw a copy of her book, it was so evident that everything in it was slanted, twisted, or was a bald-faced lie. She could not get anything right. She even misquoted the KJV.

Everyone who has objectively investigated her NEW AGE BIBLE VERSIONS book has said virtually everything in the book is a misquotation, is misleading, is an error or is unsubstantiated statements.

David Cloud is a strong believer in the KJV Only view, but he said regarding **NEW AGE VERSIONS,** "It is the frequent error in documentation, in logic, and in statement of fact that gives cause for alarm. There are many good points made in the book, but it is so marred by error, carelessness, and faulty logic that it cannot be used as a dependable resource." Cloud went on to say that the book was not accurate in its references, the documentation was unreliable and it contained countless statements which were entirely unsubstantiated.

Riplinger claimed she was inspired by God to write her book. She said it was such a direct revelation from God, she hesitated to put her name on it. So she put G. A. Riplinger, which meant to her, God as the author and Riplinger as secretary. So she is saying that God is the primary author.

The Bible clearly says inspiration stopped when Revelation chapter 22 was complete. Riplinger is doing the same thing cults do when they add their books to the Bible. Gail Riplinger is a heretic. She is not worthy to be taken seriously. Yet thousands read what she says and do not question it. This is amazing!

How can someone with the degrees and training which Mrs. Riplinger is supposed to have, make such mistakes? The answer is this. Mrs. Riplinger is not a Bible scholar. All of her degrees, her teaching, and her writing had been in the area of interior design. When she taught at Kent State, it was in the Home Economics department. She taught interior design.

NAMES OF KJV ONLY BOOKS

Just the names of these crazy KJV Only books show the lack of logic the movement is built on. One is called THE FINAL AUTHORITY. Everybody should know the original Hebrew and Greek is the final authority. However, the purpose of this book is to show the KJV is the final authority. Another book is GOD WROTE ONLY ONE BIBLE. Of course God only wrote one Bible but the book tries to show God only wrote one version, which is entirely a different matter. But KJV Only folks don't see the stretch here: the change from Bible to *version.*

Another book is THINGS THAT ARE DIFFERENT ARE NOT THE SAME. The argument of this book attempts to tell readers that if something is different, it cancels whatever it differs with. That is faulty logic. A Ford and a Cadillac are different but one does not cancel the other. Both will carry you where you want to go. They both serve the same purpose. So Bible versions are different but they serve the same purpose. One version may be in old English, another in Modern English, but both serve the same purpose. KJV Only people can't see this. Another book is, LET'S WEIGH THE EVIDENCE but the only evidence given is one sided and the only thing it proves is the lack of logic of the author. Is Logic and common sense being abandoned by modern preachers and Christians?

WORD FOR WORD TRANSLATION?

The KJV Only group is so against dynamic equivalency (This term means that translators give the meaning, rather than a word for word translation). They contend the KJV is a word for word translation. Actually there is no such thing possible. All translators know this.

Among Bible scholars it is well known that the KJV translators used many words to translate just one Hebrew or Greek word. The Hebrew for "word" or "thing" is rendered by eighty-four separate English words. The Hebrew word for "face" uses thirty-four English words. For the Hebrew word "sim", they used fifty-nine English words. The Hebrew word for "good" uses forty-one words to translate it. To translate the Hebrew word for "much" or "many" the KJV translators used forty-four words. The Hebrew term for "turn back" uses sixty English words.

On the other hand, the KJV sometimes uses only one English word to translate many original words. "Vex" appears 37 times as a translation for 23 different Hebrew or Greek terms. The word "vile" is used to translate 9 different Hebrew words. The word "ordain" is used to translate 10 different Hebrew words and 12 different Greek words.

The expression "God forbid" is found about 12 times in the KJV Old Testament, but the Hebrew text which is being translated has no reference to Deity. The Hebrew exclamation which the KJV translators translated "God forbid" means something to be rejected immediately and decisively.

The phrase "God forbid" is found about 14 times in the KJV New Testament. It is found throughout Paul's epistles. However, the word "God" is not found in the Greek in any of these places. This expression is used ten times in the book of Romans alone. Examples are Romans 3:4, 6, 31; 6:2, 15. This phrase in the Greek means "may it never be" or "Certainly not." "God forbid" does convey the thought of the Greek, but it is not a word for word translation.

The Godly Hebrew people would never use a term like "God forbid." To them it would be almost blasphemy. They would consider it taking God's name in vain. Some Old Testament scribes would not even write the name of God in the manuscripts. They would leave the space blank.

In the Old Testament the phrase "God save the king" is used about five times. In none of these passages does the word "God" appear in the Hebrew text. It simply means, "may the king live." (Example: II Samuel 16:16)

The English people in the 1600s continually used this term, and the translators put it in here instead of translating it literally, "Let the king live."

The expression "God speed" is used in II John 10-11. In the Greek, it is the usual term for "hail" and is usually translated as "greet" or "greeting" in the modern versions. There is no corresponding word in the Greek for "God" in this verse.

All of the above examples are not literal transla- tions. The word "God" does not appear in the original in any of these verses.

The word "yet" is found in the KJV almost 700 times. In about 332 of these cases STRONG's concordance records no corresponding Hebrew or Greek word. The translators put "yet" in to make the meaning clearer or for stylistic reasons. My point is that the KJV is not always a word for word translation, as some people assert.

In Matthew 27:44 the KJV says, "They cast the same in his teeth." The Greek means they "reviled" him. There is no word for "teeth" in this Greek text. The translators used a term current in their day instead of translating it.

We see from the above examples that the KJV does contain some dynamic equivalency. It is not always a literal translation and certainly not a word for word translation.

Actually the NASB is a more literal translation than the KJV. If the KJV Only people really wanted a literal translation, they would like it but instead they curse it.

VERSES LEFT OUT?

The KJV people ask, "Why do the modern versions leave verses and words out?" I think they have the question reversed. It should be, "Why does the KJV insert so many words and verses?" The fact is, the Textus Receptus and the KJV translators included most any verse or phrase that was in any manuscript, which was available to them. The modern versions put the verse in only if the manuscript evidence required it. This is more logical. The KJV is based on the Byzantine text, which is a derived text. It obviously incorporates into itself the earlier readings found in both the Alexandrian and Western texts. When manuscripts differed, they would put in both readings. For example, in Luke 24:53 the KJV says they were "Praising and blessing God." The Alexandrian text says "blessing God." The Western text says "praising God." The Byzantine text joined both readings together rather than omitting one reading. Erasmus even put verses in out of the Latin vulgate. So there are verses and phases in the KJV that are not found in any Greek manuscript. Examples are parts of Acts 9:5-6 and Rev. 22:14. Remember it is just as bad to add to the Word as it is to delete.(Rev. 22:18)

At least when you read the modern versions you know the doubtful verses have been deleted. Therefore you know you are reading the pure word of God. When you read the KJV you may be reading a verse which is doubtful or is not in any manuscript in existence.

Actually many verses that are left out of the modern versions are repeats. For example, in Mark 9, the KJV says three times, "the fire is not quenched." The Modern versions have it only once.

Talking about adding and leaving out verses, the 1611 KJV added 14 entire books, a total of 172 chapters, called the Apocrypha. Certainly no other version adds or takes away this many verses. The 1611 KJV is the worst version of all about adding verses. How dare the KJV Only people to even talk about leaving out verses! I know Peter Ruckman and others give silly excuses and explanations for the 1611 KJV containing the Apocrypha, but the bottom line is, the original KJV contained the Apocrypha.

To be KJV Only you have to abandon all logic, ignore the facts, spin your view, slant everything in your favor, and have the attitude, "My mind is made up. Don't bother me with the facts. They don't matter."

THE ALEXANDRIAN TEXT

Peter Ruckman says that anything that comes from Alexandria, Egypt or Rome, Italy must be wrong. Anything that comes from Antioch, Syria must be right. (See Ruckman's booklet, The Monarch of the Books) Therefore the Greek manuscripts, which came from Antioch, must be good and the ones that came from Alexandria and Rome must be bad. This is some kind of geographical prejudice. This is like saying, "Can any good thing come out of Nazareth?" Yet Christ did come from there. God does bring good things out of bad places. He brought Christ from Egypt when He was two years old. He brought Israel out of Egypt. There is no teaching in the Bible that God only brings good things from certain geographical locations.

Ruckman tries to make people believe all the heretics came from Alexandria and Rome while all the good guys came from Antioch. (CHRISTIAN HANDBOOK, p. 56-76) Yet you know that in every section within our country today, you have some of God's people and you have the cults and some in-between. Every big city has good people and bad. It has true believers and heretics. It has always been this way and it always will be. For anyone to say all the heretics were in Alexandria and Rome and all the Bible believers were in Antioch, defies all common sense. You do not have to be a church historian to know this. All you need is a brain. Just look around and tell me one place, which has all good or all bad.

Church history shows that Antioch, Rome and Alexandria each had Bible believers and heretics, just like every other place.

The reason why most scholars believe the Alexandrian and Vatican manuscripts are good is because they are older. Which means they were copied less. When the originals were written, a copy was made. Then a copy of the copy was made. Then a copy of the last copy was made, and so on. Errors occurred during this process. The manuscripts, which came from Alexandria and

Rome, go back so far they could have been copied directly from the originals. We don't know that they were, but certainly they were copied less times than the much later manuscripts used for the Textus Receptus, from which we get the KJV.

In other words, the Alexandrian Manuscripts are the oldest, while only later manuscripts support the Textus Receptus text. The argument against the early manuscripts by the KJV Only cult is they are weak on the deity of Christ. We showed in chapter three that this is not true. The NIV, translated from these manuscripts, is stronger on the deity of Christ than the KJV translated from the later manuscripts.

WESTCOTT AND HORT

B.F. Westcott and F.J.A. Hort are the main scholars the KJV Only advocates love to hate. Gail Riplinger and others have misquoted and misinterpreted what they said. They even quote W.W. Westcott and attribute it to the scholar B.F. Westcott. Riplinger and others quote B.F. Westcott's son when he said his father has investigated spiritualism. They use this against Westcott. They fail to give the conclusion his son wrote, "such investigations led to no good."

Dr. Stewart Custer in his book, THE KING JAMES CONTROVERSY, gives three pages of quotes from the books of Westcott and Hort showing conclusively they were Christians and Bible believing scholars. He shows they believed the Bible was the Word of God. They believed in the deity of Christ; the virgin birth; the blood atonement; that personal faith in Christ is what saves; Christ is the creator and Lord of all; His one sacrifice is complete and sufficient, etc.

If one wants to continue to believe Westcott and Hort were apostates, that is up to them. However, the facts show Westcott and Hort were Bible believing Christians. Yes, they believed in sprinkling babies and in other rituals of the Church of England. But remember the KJV translators were members of the same church and believed the same doctrines as Westcott and Hort. If the KJV translators did not believe what the church of England stood for, they were hypocrites to remain in it. So many people brag about the King James translators being so smart and knowledgeable. If they were so smart, why did they belong to the Church of England? Why were they not Baptist? The Fact is, King James and the Church of England hated Baptists.

ANTI-BAPTIST KJV

It is well known that King James hated Baptists. He said he wanted to "harrow out of England" all Baptists. The King James Version was rejected by Baptists when it first came out. When the Baptists first came to America, they brought the Geneva Bible, not the KJV. In fact, some of the first Baptists to arrive here had been run out of England by King James.

King James, in 1612, imprisoned a Baptist preacher named Thomas Helwys for a tract he had written opposing the state church (Church of England).

John Bunyan, a Baptist and author of PILGRIMS PROGRESS, spent many years in the Bedford prison because of persecution from the Church of England (which King James and the KJV translators were part of).

CHAPTER 8

In the early days of this country, when the Anglican church (Church of England) was the state
church in Virginia, they persecuted, imprisoned and
beat many Baptists. Thomas Jefferson, the second
governor of the state, made religious persecution
illegal. But when they had the power, the Church of
England and King James hated and persecuted
Baptists. Yet today, many Baptists want to idolize
this Baptist hating king.

The KJV translators, when they presented their
new translation to the King, said he was as "the sun
shining in its strength."(Dedicatory To The Most
High and Mighty Prince, James. Page 1 of the 1611
KJV) Of course, this expression in the Bible refers
to the Lord Jesus Christ. Many people today, like
the KJV translators, would exalt King James to a
place he could never deserve.

PRO CATHOLIC

A heavy Catholic influence was exhibited in the
KJV from the time of Erasmus, a Roman Catholic
who compiled the Greek text. The reason he put I
John 5:7 in his Greek text was because the Catholic
church threatened to excommunicate him if he
didn't. This verse is found in only two late Greek
manuscripts. It is not found in the Majority text.
Erasmus knew it did not belong in his Greek text.
But the worst thing to a Catholic is ex-
communication, so he put it in. He also put in other
verses from the Latin Roman Catholic Bible.

The Church of England was started by Henry VIII
because he wanted to divorce and re-marry.
Catholics do not allow this, so King Henry left the
Catholic church and started the Church of England.
He made it the state church. Of course, his church

was patterned after the Catholic church. Remember most of the KJV translators were members of the Church of England. This is why they have a page for a holy day in front of the 1611 KJV dedicated to the "blessed Virgin." This is the reason they refused to translate the Greek words for "baptism" and "deacon." They transliterated them. This means they just spelled them out in English. If they had translated them, it would have conflicted with their practice of sprinkling instead of baptism. "Deacon" would have to be translated as "servant" instead of the high office as the Catholics and Church of England practice it. It seems the great KJV translators were cowards and chose to bow to King James instead of doing what they knew was right.

The fact that the 1611 KJV contained the Roman Catholic Apocrypha is undeniable proof of Catholic influence. No truly Protestant or Baptist version of the Bible would contain this abomination.

CHAPTER 9

OBSOLETE WORDS IN THE KJV

There are many words in the KJV today that do not convey the meaning to the modern reader that the original writers intended to express. When the KJV came out in 1611, it was sixteenth century English at its best. Through the years many words and expressions have become ambiguous or misleading. There are hundreds of them. In this chapter I will point out samples of them. I believe the reader will find archaic and obsolete words are a much bigger problem than you would think.

ARCHAIC EXPRESSIONS

In the KJV you run into outdated expressions which the modern American could never understand without help. Of course, all of these examples I will give are updated in the NIV and the NASB.

In I Samuel 30:31 the KJV says, "Where David himself and his men were wont to haunt." Five times the KJV uses the expression, "Fetch a compass" (examples: II Sam. 5:23; Acts 28:13). In Matt. 27:44 it says, "They cast the same in his teeth." In Mark 9:18 the KJV says, "And pineth away." In Gal. 4:24 it says, "Which gendereth to bondage, which is Agar." In James 1:21 we are told to "lay apart all filthiness and superfluity of naughtiness."

The reader will never know what these obsolete expressions mean unless he looks them up in another source. The NIV or the NASB makes them all simple enough so a child can understand them.

To those who argue for the beautiful and lofty language of the KJV, I will challenge you to go out in public and talk in King James English today. You will soon see how odd and outdated it is. Try it. I dare you! Of course you will not do it because you do not want to sound silly. But you don't care if God does.

Now let us focus on some of the words in the KJV that have changed or taken on new meanings through the years.

ARCHAIC WORDS

ADMIRE, ADMIRATION was used in 1611 to denote wonder or astonishment, without any implication of praise or approval. That is why John in Rev. 17:6 looks at the great Whore, which is the mother of harlots and abominations of the earth, and "wondered with great admiration." Of course, John did not admire this wicked woman but he was amazed and wondered. The NIV says," I was greatly astonished." The KJV conveys the wrong meaning here and in other places where these words are used.

AFFINITY means nearness of kin or mutual attraction today. The Hebrew word translated "affinity" by the KJV means, "relationship by marriage, especially by a father and a son-in-law." In 2 Chronicles 18:1 Jehoshaphat "joined affinity with Ahab." In Ezra 9:14 the KJV says, "Should we again break thy commandments, and join in affinity with the people of these abominations." The NASB says "intermarry" or "allied himself by marriage." The reader of the KJV will miss part of the meaning in these verses while the NASB makes it clear.

AGAINST today means opposite or confronting. Notice how it is used in the KJV. In Genesis 43:25, "against Joseph came" and Exodus 7:15 it says, "against he come" and in II Kings 16:11, "against king Ahaz came." In Numbers 25:4 it says, "Take the heads of the people and hang them up before the LORD against the sun." Over and over the KJV uses the word "against" when another word would give a clearer meaning for the modern reader. The NIV and the NASB usually say "for" or "before" in these passages.

AGONE is an outdated word for "ago." In I Samuel the Egyptian said, "Three days agone I fell sick."(30:13) The NASB says, "I fell sick three days ago."

ALLEGE today means merely to assert. In the sixteenth century it meant to produce evidence and to prove. In Acts 17, Paul for three Sabbaths reasoned with the Jews out of the Scriptures. Verse 3 says, "Opening and alleging, that Christ must needs have suffered, and risen again from the dead." Does anyone believe that Paul only asserted but did not prove and give evidence for what he said? The NASB says, "Explaining and giving evidence."

ALWAY appears 23 times in the KJV and "always" 62 times. Today we always add the "s." In Titus 1:12 Paul said, "The Cretians are alway liars." Matthew 28:20 says, "Lo, I am with you alway."

ANGLE meant "fishhook" to the KJV translators. "All they who cast angle into the brooks" means "all those who cast a hook into the Nile." (Isa. 19:8 NIV) The KJV turned around and translated the same word as "hook" in Job 41:1. "Canst thou draw out leviathan with an hook?"

ANON means "soon" or "presently" in my dictionary today. The Greek word translated "anon" means "immediately" or "straightway." The KJV can be misleading here. For example, in Mark 1:30, when Jesus entered Peter's house they immediately tell Him about the sick mother-in-law. However, the KJV says that "anon" they told Him. This makes it sound like they waited awhile. The stony ground hearer in the parable of the sower heard the word and "anon with joy receiveth it." (Matt. 13:20-21) The Greek says he received it immediately while the KJV makes it sound like he might have waited awhile. I realize this is no big deal. But the point I want to make is that throughout the KJV, in small things as well as the big, the reader is being misled.

APOTHECARY appears six times in the KJV. The word means one who prepares and sells drugs for medicine. However, the Hebrew word means "perfumer." The NASB always says "perfumer."

ARMHOLE is used for "armpit" in the KJV. In Ezekiel 13:18 it says, "Sew pillows to all armholes." In Jeremiah 38:12 it says, "Put now these old cast clouts and rotten rags under thine armholes under the cords." The NASB says, "Now put these worn-out clothes and rags under your armpits under the ropes." Anyone can see that "armpit" is better than "armhole." I am not sure what an "armhole" is, unless it is a hole in your arm.

AT is used in an obsolete way in Exodus 19:15. It says, "Come not at your wives." Numbers 6:6 tells the nazarite, "he shall come at no dead body." The Hebrew means don't come near your wives or near any dead body. I give only two examples here, but many times the KJV uses "at" in the obsolete sense.

AWAY WITH is an old expression used in Isaiah 1:13. "I cannot away with." The Hebrew means tolerate or endure. The NASB says, "I cannot endure." This expression, which we never use today, makes it harder for the reader to see that God cannot endure false religion.

BAKEMEATS is used in Genesis 40:17, where the chief baker was carrying "all manner of bakemeats for Pharaoh." This simply means all sorts of food prepared by a baker, (which usually contained no meat). It has little to do with the modern conception of baked meats.

BEAST is used in the KJV as a general term for all living creatures other than man. The word "animal" is not used in the KJV. The word "reptile" does not appear, since it is was not in current use then.

The word "beast" is used in the book of Revelation to refer to the holy living creatures around the throne of God. (4:6,7,8) Remarkably, the same word is used to refer to the wicked "beast" that rises out of the sea, and the "beast" that rises out of the bottomless pit. (13:1,11; 17:8) There are two different Greek words used in these passages. One means "living creatures" and the other means "wild beasts." The KJV makes no distinction. The NASB does.

BESOM is an outdated word for broom. In Isaiah 14:23, God says of Babylon, "I will sweep it with the besom of destruction."

BETHINK THEMSELVES is used in I Kings 8:47, "Yet if they shall bethink themselves in the land." The NASB says, "If they take thought in the land."

BETIMES means early or in time. However, the Hebrew word the KJV translates as "betimes" actually means diligent or persistent. In II Chronicles 36:15 when the Lord sent messengers "betimes," it means He sent them persistently. In Proverbs 13:24 the KJV says chasten him "be-

times." It actually means to "discipline him diligently." This word "betimes" in the KJV, misled me
in my early Christian life. The reader should
research every verse where the word is used before
he assumes he knows the meaning of it.

BEWRAY is an obsolete word which meant to
reveal or disclose. In Matthew 26:73, Peter was
told, "thy speech bewrayeth thee." The NIV says,
"Your accent gives you away." I believe "bewray" is
used about four times in the KJV.

BLOW UP is used in the KJV sometimes instead
of simply "blow." In Psalm 81:3, it says, "Blow up
the trumpet." Today "blow up" means to explode or
inflate.

BOLLED is used in the KJV in Exodus 9:31. It
says "the flax was bolled." The Hebrew word
means bud or bloom. Of course, the NASB or the
NIV brings this out.

BOTCH, as used by the KJV, is an archaic word
that means boils or sores, as the "botch of Egypt",
etc.

BOWELS is used 28 times in the Old Testament.
Sometimes the word is used literally as we would
use it today. In II Samuel 20:10, Joab cut out the
"bowels" of Amasa. The NASB says, "inward
parts," which sounds better.

Also, the KJV uses the word "bowels" to denote
the womb and the male organs. This can be misleading. In about 10 instances the word "bowels" is
used for feelings and emotions. Examples: "My
bowels are troubled." (Lam. 1:20) "My bowels were
moved for him." (S.S. 5:4) The KJV says of Joseph
that "his bowels did yearn upon his brother." (Gen.
43:30)

In eight passages in the New Testament the KJV uses "bowels" in the sense of affection or compassion. The Greek word does not refer to the intestines specifically, but to the "inward parts." It is much like the word for heart, which can mean your blood pump, or it can mean "inward affection" or "sincere emotion" (As, "I love you with all my heart.") In the English language of 1611, both "bowels" and "heart" had this double reference to physical organs and to emotions of which these organs were supposed to be the seat. Today only the word "heart" retains the double meaning.

When Paul tells the Philippians that he longs for them "in bowels of Jesus Christ" (1:8), he means the affections of Jesus Christ. In Colossians 3:12, Paul talks about "bowels of mercies." In I John 3:17 the KJV says, "shutteth up his bowels of compassion from him." The book of Philemon uses "bowels" about three times. This book will mean more if you put "heart" in the place of "bowels." In fact, the many passages where the word "bowels" is used, will mean more if you will read them in the NIV or the NASB.

The word "bowels" was a good word in 1611, but I would not recommend that you use it in polite society today. It is a very crude word now. It should be updated.

BULLOCK is used today only of bulls that have been castrated. In the KJV the word means a young bull. To use the word "bullock" today is a blatant mistranslation because the word means something different than it did in 1611. The Bible says the bull had to be without blemish to be offered to the Lord.

CARE, CAREFULNESS, CAREFUL are words that can be misunderstood by the readers of the KJV.

They appear in the sense of anxiety or worry. Martha was "careful and troubled about many things." (Luke 10:41) This means she was worried and upset. Paul told the Corinthians, "I would have you without carefulness." (I Cor. 7:32) This means that Paul wanted them free from worry or anxiety. God does not want His children to worry. (Phil. 4:6 NASB) The reader can miss some blessings unless he refers to another version where these obsolete words are not used.

CARRIAGE in the KJV means that which is carried. Today it means a vehicle by which persons or things are carried, such as a horse and carriage. I still remember as a young Christian, I read, "we took up our carriages and went to Jerusalem."(Acts 21:15) I did not understand then, "that they took up their baggage."

CERTIFY today means to attest or declare by a formal or legal certificate. The KJV uses the word "certify" when the meaning is simply to tell or to make known. Examples: "Esther certified the king thereof." (Esther 2:22) In Galatians 1:11, Paul says, "I certify you brethren." In neither case is there any implication of formal attestation. The Greek means "to make known" or "I would have you to know."

CHOLER is an outdated word that once meant anger. In Daniel 8:7, "He was moved with choler." In 11:11, "The king of the south shall be moved with choler." The Hebrew word means he was enraged or moved with anger. We do not use the old word "choler" today. If you did, no one would know what you meant.

CLOSET is used several times in the KJV. The word once meant a private room but this is not the meaning today. Sometimes the KJV translators use "chamber" for the same word. The Greek word for "closet" means private room or storeroom. "Closet" is ambiguous in Matthew 6:6, where it says, "enter into thy closet, and when thou hast shut the door, pray to thy Father which is in secret." The reader is misled in all other places where the word closet is used.

COLLEGE is a mistranslation of the Hebrew word which means the second quarter or district. The KJV says Huldah the prophetess "dwelt in Jerusalem in the college." (II Kings 22:14; II Chron. 34:22) The NIV says, "in the Second District." The word "college" has misled me before I learned better.

OBSOLETE WORDS IN THE KJV
PART 2

Imagine what it would be like to talk to someone in the 1600s. They had never heard of electricity. It would be hard to make them understand when you try to talk to them about television, computers, microwave ovens, laser beams, jet planes and rockets to Mars. This is the kind of problem we have trying to read old outdated English today.

This chapter is a continuation of the previous chapter. We are discussing archaic words in the KJV.

COMPEL is used incorrectly several times in the KJV. King Saul's servants did not "compel" him to eat but they "urged" him. (I Sam. 28:23) The KJV translators used "urge" or "press" for the same Hebrew word in other places. Paul, before his conversion, did not "compel" the early Christians to blaspheme. He tried to make them do so. (Acts 26:11) Both the NIV and the NASB say, "I tried to force them to blaspheme." This makes more sense of course, because one cannot force a Christian to blaspheme. One can only try.

CONFECTION, CONFECTIONARY are words which now refer to candy and sweet things, which taste good to eat because of their sugar content. In the KJV, these words refer to things that smell good, like perfume or incense. An example is I Samuel 8:13. Here the people were told the king would take their daughters to be "confectionaries." The word means "perfumers," not sweet things.

CONVERSATION in the KJV always refers to conduct, behavior, or the way you live. In 1611 it was never used in the sense that we use it today;

meaning talk back and forth. This outdated word misleads the reader in many places.

COUSIN in the KJV simply means a relative or kinsman, and not a "cousin" as we use the word today. The angel told Mary that her "cousin" Elizabeth had conceived a son. The Greek word means "kinswoman." When Elizabeth gave birth to John the Baptist, it was her neighbors and "kins-folk" that rejoiced with her, not her neighbors and "cousins," as the KJV says in Luke 1:58. Also, the Greek word that describes Mark's relation to Barnabas does not mean "sister's son", as the KJV says but it means "cousin." (Col. 4:10) The KJV has the word "cousin" where it shouldn't be and where it should be "cousin" they put the wrong word.

CREATURE sometimes means the whole created universe or it can mean anything created, in the KJV. To use "creature" this way is now obsolete. (Romans 8:19-21,39) In II Cor. 5:17 where it says we are a "new creature," it really means a "new creation."

CURIOUS once meant made with care and skill. The "curious girdle of the ephod" was a "skillfully woven band to gird it on."(Ex. 28:8) "Curiously wrought in the lowest parts of the earth" is better translated "skillfully wrought" or "woven together." (Psalm 139:15) This same Hebrew word is some-times translated "embroidered." Of course, the word curious does not have that meaning today.

In the New Testament "curious" is used in Acts 19:19. It says, "Many of them also which used curious arts brought their books together, and burned them." The NASB says, "And many of those who practiced magic brought their books together and began to burn them." We do not use the word "curious" to describe the occult or magic today.

DELICACY and DELICIOUSLY are used in Revelation 18 in the archaic sense of sensual luxury. In this chapter, God is judging "Babylon the great" for the abundance of her "delicacies."(vs.3) But the word does not refer to an abundant supply of dainties but to the "wealth of her sensual luxury." The kings who "lived deliciously with her" were indulging their lust and greed. (vs. 9) So we see that "delicacy" and "deliciously" do not accurately convey the meaning of the Greek.

DEMAND means to ask with authority or to request something as a right or request urgently. However, as used in the KJV, it does not have the stronger connotations. It simply means to "ask." "Demand" in the KJV does not mean the same as it means to us today.

DEPUTY today means a person appointed to act for another, or one elected to represent a constituency. The word "deputy" should be "governor" or "proconsul" about 25 times in the KJV. The NASB and the NIV make the necessary changes in these passages.

DESCRY means to get sight of, investigate or spy on. It is used in Judges 1:23, "the house of Joseph sent to descry Bethel." When I saw this word for the first time in this passage, I had no idea what it meant. The NIV says, 'they sent men to spy out Bethel." That I can understand.

DISANNUL means annul, abolish or cancel. The NIV and the NASB simply delete the prefix "dis." Annul is easier for the modern reader.

DIVERS and DIVERSE were originally two spellings of the same word. But each word developed it's own pronunciation and meaning. "Diverse" meant "different in character or quality." "Divers" meant "various, sundry, more than one," I believe the word "diverse" is used 8 times and the word "divers" is used about 36 times in the KJV. Of course, we seldom use these words today.

EAR and plow once had the same meanings. Today "ear" does not mean to prepare the soil for sowing, as plowing does. The KJV, in many places, uses the word "ear" meaning getting the ground ready for seeding. Genesis 45:6 says, "There shall neither be earing nor harvest." Exodus 34:21 says, "in earing time and in harvest." I Samuel 8:12 says, "to ear his ground." The NASB and the NIV do not use the word "ear," because it has a different meaning today.

EMERODS is an old word for hemorrhoids or piles. These three words were used interchangeably until the seventeenth century but only the word "emerods" is used in the KJV. All but one of the appearances of this word are in the account of the plague which smote the Philistines when they had captured the ark of the LORD. (I Samuel 5-6). There is no good reason to translate the Hebrew word by "emerods." To do so is complicated by the fact the Philistines made imitations of the emerods. I would imagine it would be hard to make a likeness of hemorrhoids. Everything is clearer if you translate the word as "tumors," as the NASB does.

FAST means close or near in the KJV. This is an inaccurate meaning today. Ruth 2:8 says, "abide here fast by my maidens." Ruth 2:21,23 says, "Thou shalt keep fast by my young men." "So she kept fast by the maidens of Boaz." The NASB says, "stay close" instead of "fast." This translation is easier to understand for the modern reader.

GENERATION today means the whole body of individuals born about the same time period; also the time covered by the lives of these. The KJV gives "generation" a different meaning in Matthew 1:1, "The generation of Jesus Christ." There the Greek word is "genesis," a different word from the one usually translated "generation." The KJV translates a totally different Greek word in I Peter 2:9 as, "a chosen *generation*." In Greek this word means a chosen race. When John the Baptist and Jesus said, "generation of vipers" that is yet another Greek word. This word means, "offspring or brood of vipers." The reader of the KJV would do well to check another source to find the true meaning in the verses containing "generation."

GOODMAN is a husband or the male head of a household. The word is now archaic. In Proverbs 7:19, a harlot tells her prospect, "the goodman is not at home." The NIV says, "My husband is not at home." Five times in the Gospels it speaks of the "Goodman of the house."

HAPLY is used about 6 times in the KJV, I believe. It is an outdated word that meant "perchance" or "perhaps."

LIST means to desire or wish. The KJV says, "the wind bloweth where it listeth." (John 3:8) "Whatsoever they listed." (Matt. 17:12) I believe "list" is used four times. It is now archaic.

MINISH is old English for become less. Pharaoh tells the Hebrews in Exodus 5:19, "Ye shall not minish ought from your bricks of your daily task." Psalm 107:39 says, "they are minished and brought low." The NASB says, "they are diminished and bowed down."

NAUGHT means "bad" in the KJV. Proverbs 20:14 says, "It is naught, it is naught, saith the buyer." "The water is naught." (II Kings 2:19) The NASB and the NIV say "bad" or "no good."

NEESING is an obsolete word for sneezing. In Job 41:18 it says, "By his neesing a light doth shine."

RUDE once meant unskilled. When Paul said, "I be rude in speech." (II Cor.11:6) He meant he was not an expert, not a professional orator.

SEETHE, SOD, SODDEN is old English meaning to cook food by boiling or stewing. Sod and sodden are the past tense of "seethe." For an example, see 1 Samuel 2:13,15. Of course we do not use these words today.

SHAMBLES means "meat market' in the KJV. Today "shambles' would be used to describe a place that was wrecked, as a room full of broken things in disarray.

When we read the word "shambles" we think we know the meaning. However, the word has changed meaning over the years. This is the worst thing about obsolete words. In many instances you think you know the meaning so you do not look for another. Thus, the words are misleading. We think we understand but we do not. This happens over and over when reading the KJV today. I know. It has happened to me many times.

SORE in the KJV means severe, intense or very great. The word is used almost a hundred times. Examples are: "sore war", "the battle was sore", "sore wounded", "sore afraid." We do not speak this way today.

SOTTISH meant foolish or stupid in 1611. Jeremiah 4:22 says, "they are sottish children." We do not use that word today.

TIRE has nothing to do with fatigue, or with wheels, as used in the KJV. It is a shortened form of "attire." Ezekiel 24:17 says, "bind the tire of thine head upon thee." The NASB says, "bind on your turban." The same Hebrew word is translated by the KJV as "bonnet", "beauty" and "ornaments." We do not use the word "tire" today in this outdated sense.

TUTOR means "guardian" in the KJV. Today it means "teacher." Galations 4:2 says that the heir is "under tutors and governors." The NASB says he is "under guardians and managers." Actually the word "tutors" and the word "governor" are obsolete as used in the KJV.

VISAGE meant "face" in 1611. When the KJV says Nebuchadnezzar's visage was changed, it means his face was changed. (Daniel 3:19) In Isaiah 52:14 the suffering Saviour's "visage was so marred." The NASB says, "His appearance was marred." I don't think we use "visage" today.

WAKE is used in the KJV for "awake." Psalm 127:1 says, "the watchman waketh but in vain." The NASB says, "The watchman keeps awake in vain." "Wake" today means watch over the dead or staying up with the dead. We use the word "wake" today but not as a substitute for "awake" as the KJV does.

WHICH is used in the KJV for persons as well as for things. Examples are: "Lot also, which went with Abram."(Gen. 13:5) " a new king over Egypt, which knew not Joseph."(Exodus 1:8) "Thanks be to God, which giveth us the victory." (I Cor.15:57)

"Which" is used about 177 times and refers to persons about 37 times. Of course this is bad grammar today. The KJV contains much bad grammar besides the use of "which." The words "who" and "whom" are used in the KJV many times. But even in the Lord's prayer it says, "Our Father which art in heaven." Of course the NASB says, "Our Father who art in heaven." (Matt. 6:9)

WHILES, WHILST are old English words for "while." The KJV uses the word "whiles" about 10 times and "whilst" about 9 times, but "while" is used about 200 times. There is no difference in the meaning of these three terms. Of course we do not use the first two words today.

WIT, WIST, WOT once meant to know or to find out. "Wot" is present tense and "wist" is past tense. Exodus 2:4 gives an example of "wit." "His sister stood afar off, to wit what would be done to him." "Wist" is used in Luke 2:49, "Wist ye not that I must be about my Father's business." "Wot" is used in Gen. 21:26. "I wot not who hath done this thing."

The expression "to wit" has been inserted in the KJV about 16 times, without any corresponding Hebrew or Greek words. This was to try to make the meaning clearer.

WITHAL is an obsolete form of "with." A typical passage is Job 2:8, "he took him a potsherd to scrape himself withal." This means he took a potsherd to scrape himself with.

There is another word that is used 8 times in the KJV but I cannot print it here. It was a good word in 1611 but has taken on a vulgar meaning today. The NIV translates it "urine" or "male." The reader can check out these references if he is interested:

II Kings 18:27; Isaiah 36:12; I Samuel 25:22,34; I Kings 14:10; II Kings 9:8; 16:11; 21:21

CONCLUSION

I have given some samples of archaic and obsolete words found in the KJV. This is by no means all of them. Some scholars have listed over 800 outdated words. If you multiply the number of archaic words by the number of times each one is used, you have an astronomical number of words that can mislead the reader or make it hard or impossible to understand what God actually said. The whole purpose of a translation is to make the Word of God clear. The KJV translators believed this. I firmly believe, if they were alive today, they would be among the first to recommend updating the old KJV.

The worst problem with Archaic words is, that they are misleading because the word has changed it's meaning over the years. So you read it and come away with a different message than what God actually said. Examples are: nephew, shipping, against, admire, prevent, replenish, etc.

How many of us have read Genesis 1:28, where God said, "Be fruitful and multiply and replenish the earth," and we thought there must have been someone here before Adam and Eve because we know what "replenish" means. However, today the word has changed meaning and has nothing to do with renewing a diminished supply. It simply means to fill. This type thing happens over and over when you are reading obsolete words. The KJV is full of them.

MORE EXAMPLES OF OBSOLETE WORDS TO WATCH OUT FOR

I want to give another list of outdated words for those who might still be unconvinced that obsolete words are a problem in the KJV. I will give only one reference with each word.

Let me again warn the reader that the words you think you understand, are the most dangerous. The meaning of words you may know has probably changed. The message it conveys today is different than the meaning it had when the KJV was written. Keep this in mind as you look over the list below.

Chambering. Rom. 13:13
Champaign. Deut. 11:30
Stomacher. Isaiah 3:4
Suretiship. Prov. 11:15
Amerce. Deut 22:19
Brigadine. Jere. 46:4
Withs. Judges 16:7
Wen. Lev. 22:22
Target. I Sam. 17:6
Strange women. I Kings 11:1
Leasing. Psalm 5:6
All to. Judges 9:53
Ark. Exodus 2:3
Assay. I Sam. 17:39
Astonied. Ezra 9:3
Audience. Gen. 23:10
Bestead. Isa. 8:21
Blain. Exodus 9:9
Bruit. Jere. 10:22
Canker. II Tim. 2:17
Chapt. Jere. 14:4
Clean. Josh. 4:11
Conceit. Prov. 26:5

Creek. Acts 27:39
Dayspring. Job 38:12
Decay. Job 14:11
Diet. Jere. 52:33-34
Discover. Lamentations 2:14
Doctor. Luke 2:46
Dure. Matt. 13:21
Ensample. I Cor 10:1
Fain. Lluke 15:16
Familiar spirit. Lev. 20:27
Fashion. Exodus 26:20
Fetch about. II Sam. 14:20
Flood. Joshua 24:2
Flowers. Lev. 15:24
Flux. Acts 28:8
For to. Mark 3:10
Fray. Deut. 28:26
Fret. Lev. 13:51
Garnish. II Chron. 3:6
Gin. Psalm 140:5
Grudge. James 5:9
Hap. Ruth 2:3
Hereunto. I Peter 2:21
Hold. Judges 9:46
Holden. Prov. 5:22
Hough. Joshua 11:6
Howbeit. Judges 18:29
Implead. Acts 19:38
Intelligence. Dan. 11:30
Inward. Job 19:19
Knop. I Kings 6:18
Libertines. Acts 6:9
Lucre. I Sam. 8:3
Mean. Isa. 2:9
Meteyard. Lev. 19:35

Motions. Rom. 7:5
Munition. Isaiah 33:16
Occurrent. I Kings 5:4
Offend. Matt. 13:41
Ouches. Exodus 28:II
Outlandish. Neh. 13:26
Paps. Luke 11:27
Peculiar. Titus 2:14
Post. II Chron. 30:6
Prey. Joshua 8:2
Privily. Matt. 1:19
Record. Deut. 30:19
Reins. Exodus 29:132
Require. Ezra 8:22
Shamefacedness. I Tim.2:9
Sincere. I Peter 2:2
Singular. Lev. 27:2
Sith. Ezek. 35:6
Sottish. Jere. 4:22
Stand Upon. I Sam. 1:9
Straiten. Jere. 19:9
Surfeiting. Luke 21:34
Tabering. Nahum 2:6-7
Taken with the manner. Num. 5:13
Tender eyed. Gen. 29:17
Trow. Luke 17:9
Unicorn. Job 39:9
Woe Worth. Ezek. 30:2
Waster. Prov. 18:9
Wealth. I Cor. 10:24
Whereabout. I Sam. 21:2
Whereinsoever. II Cor. 11:21
Will. Judges 1:14

FINAL ARGUMENTS

Perhaps there are still some questions in the minds of some people because of things they have heard or books they have read. In this chapter I want to answer arguments and objections that the KJV Only advocates raise for using only the KJV and for rejecting all other versions. On the following pages I outline some of the arguments for having a KJV Only view, and I give my response to each argument. I will give the KJV argument in bold print each time and my response will follow.

IF YOU REJECT THE KJV ONLY VIEW, YOU HAVE NO FINAL SCRIPTURAL AUTHORITY.

Nothing could be further from the truth. Peter Ruckman's silly Alexandrian Cult creed asserts this objection, but it is nonsense. I believe, like the KJV translators, that all translations are the Word of God. Those who translated the King James Bible did not have such a narrow view as Peter Ruckman or the KJV Only group. They did not believe a translation had to be perfect to be called the Word of God. They said, "The meanest translation is the Word of God." This is what I believe. I also believe the originals were the inspired Word. We have thousands of copies of it, counting manuscripts, versions in other languages, and the quotations from church fathers. We are rich and blessed with the authoritative Word of God.

SATAN IS BEHIND THE NEW VERSIONS OF THE BIBLE.

Gail Riplinger claims her book documents the hidden alliance between new Bible versions and the New Age Movement's One World Religion. She alleges that these new versions prepare the apostate church of the last days to accept the Anti-Christ, his mark, his image and his religion, which is Lucifer worship. Riplinger's book is full of conspiracy theories, which she does not prove. Her book consists of lies, slander, misrepresentation, and wild imagination, from the first page until the last. Why anyone would take it seriously, I cannot see.

If Satan is behind the NIV or NASB, he has not changed any of their teachings. Every doctrine found in the KJV is also found in these versions. Every teaching found in the NIV or NASB is found in the KJV and vice versa. So if Satan is behind one he is behind all.

The Revised Standard Version is notorious for leaving out the virgin birth in Isaiah 7:14. Still the virgin birth is taught in this translation in Matt. 1:23, and long passages like Luke 1:26-37 and Matthew 1:18-25. The point is, that even in a liberal transla-tion when the translators blatantly make changes, the doctrines remain intact. Remember, all Bible teachings are mentioned over and over. I do not justify any changes. I am simply making a point.

MODERN TRANSLATIONS REFER TO JOSEPH AS THE FATHER OF CHRIST.

Yes, but so does the King James Version. See Luke 2:27,41,48. (KJV) There Mary and Joseph are called his parents and Mary calls Joseph Jesus' father. Of course he was the legal father, but not the biological father.

MODERN TRANSLATIONS DO NOT USE "THEE" AND "THOU" WHEN ADDRESSING GOD.

The Greek does not have special pronouns for God. Hebrew does not have special pronouns for addressing God. The KJV does not have them either. Of course, the KJV uses "thee" and "thou" but it uses them for everybody. The KJV has no special pronouns used only for God. No one in the Bible used them, including the Lord Jesus Christ. Why should we? It is tradition, plain and simple. There is no Scripture or reason for doing so.

WESTCOTT AND HORT WERE LIBERALS AND THE MODERN VERSIONS CAME FROM THEIR GREEK TEXTS.

The modern versions do not slavishly follow these two men. The NIV and the NASB follow an eclectic text, which means they take into consideration all Greek manuscripts.

I do not believe all the lies and slander told about Westcott and Hort. I do not believe they were extreme liberals. The Christian thing to do is never believe anything bad about a brother or sister until it is conclusively proven. (I Tim. 5:19) To do so is a sin. The only thing that really matters about Westcott and Hort is whether the principles on which they drew up their Greek New Testament were valid. The greatest Greek scholars America has ever produced were firmly convinced they were. A.T. Robertson, a conservative Baptist and Gresham Machen, a conservative Presbyterian, were both defenders of the Alexandrian text and the principles on which it was based. All of the early Fundamentalists accepted it.

If we are going to reject all versions based on a Greek text prepared by liberals, then we must reject the KJV. Remember it was prepared by Erasmus, a liberal Roman Catholic, who never left the Catholic church. If all the bad things told about Westcott and Hort are true, they are still no worse than Erasmus, the man behind the Greek text of the KJV.

THE KJV HAS BEEN BLESSED BY GOD. IT HAS BROUGHT GREAT REVIVALS.

Certainly it has, but nobody knows how God will use the NIV. Already it is being blessed by God. It is outselling the KJV. Many churches using it have thousands in attendance with many being saved. Who knows what the next 400 years holds, if Jesus tarries?

However, I have never put a lot of stock in numbers or "blessings" viewed from our perspective. Consider this: Why did great revival come when backslidden Jonah preached to Nineveh, and when Jesus Christ preached they rejected and crucified Him? Which of the great prophets of the Old Testament brought revival? Isaiah, Jeremiah, Ezekiel, Amos, Malachi? None of these had revival. The original Biblical writings by the inspired apostles, did not always bring immediate revival. The saying, "The old KJV must be right because it has been blessed by God" has been blown out of proportion. Remember, for centuries the KJV was the only Bible most people had. If God was going to bless, it had to be through the KJV. The reason for the blessings was because the Bible was put into the hands of the common people for the first time.

YOU ARE TRUSTING THE SCHOLARS INSTEAD OF GOD.

Those who read the modern versions are not trusting scholars anymore than readers of the KJV. Both Greek and Hebrew texts were prepared by scholars. They were both translated into English by scholars. All of the KJV Only supporters I have met obtained their information from their scholars. The reason they are KJV Only is because they read a book or pamphlet promoting the movement. The KJV Only ideology is a manmade system. There is not one verse of Scripture, not any logic and no facts to substantiate it. It exists because one person relies on what another has said. Don't let them fool you. KJV Only believers have their libraries full of books written by their scholars. On this point, just like in most other cases, the KJV Only crowd has two sets of rules.

David Cloud, a KJV Only supporter, lists about 90 (that he called) KJV Only scholars. He was trying to prove the point that they do have many scholars in that group. (O TIMOTHY, Volume 15, Issue 3, 1998- page 11)

THE KJV IS MORE ACCURATE.

Sometimes a verse or two from the KJV is shown to be better than the same passage from a modern version. This is supposed to prove it is a more accurate translation. Certainly in some places the KJV is superior. The question is, which one is correct most of the time. No translation has all the best points. If you like the old English, choose the KJV. If you want a literal contemporary English version, choose the NASB. If you want an easy to understand modern English version, choose the NIV. I do not recommend any others because of their lack of accuracy. However, in some cases, you can use them to read along with your KJV to help you understand it better.

THE KJV IS EASIER TO MEMORIZE THAN THE MODERN TRANSLATIONS.

This is just a personal preference probably based on familiarity. At any rate, it does not prove which is more accurate. "Mary had a little lamb" is easier to memorize than the genealogies in Matthew chapter one. Does that mean that the song is more accurate? Most of us could memorize Psalm 23 easier than I Chronicles 3. Does that mean that I Chronicles 3 is less accurate?

THE NIV AND THE NASB HELPS FALSE DOC-TRINE.

No one can keep the cults from twisting verses in God's Word. The version the cults like most is the KJV, not the modern versions. More cults use the KJV than all other versions combined. Consider some of the false doctrines the KJV helps:

In I Cor. 14, the word "unknown" is inserted six times in the KJV. This has greatly helped the tongues movement. Without it, there would probably be no Charismatic or Pentecostals. The NIV and NASB do not use the word "unknown."

In Isaiah 45:7, the KJV says that God creates evil. This misleading translation can easily give people the wrong idea that God is the author of sin.

In Exodus 20:12, the KJV says, "Thou shalt not kill." The NIV and the NASB say, "You shall not murder." The KJV reading has been used to oppose capital punishment (which the Bible clearly teaches). At almost every execution, you see someone with a sign, "Thou shall not kill."

Over and over in the KJV it talks about the "end of the world." Ecc. 1:4 says, "the earth abideth for ever." There is no such thing as the end of the world as most people think of it. Jesus will come. There will be a great tribulation and a millennium, etc. But many people talk about the end of the world. This false concept comes from the KJV's mistranslation of the Greek word which means "age."

THE KJV IS BASED ON THE TEXTUS RECEPTUS AND THIS MEANS IT IS BETTER.

If that were true, it would mean that in almost 400 years, no useful manuscript has been discovered. It would mean that nothing useful has been learned about Greek in this time. That is hard to believe. It is easier to believe that just as the KJV was an improvement on Tyndale's translation, the NASB is an improvement over the KJV.

There were several different Greek New testaments used to make the KJV. All of these went through revisions before and after being used for the KJV. Are we supposed to believe that all the revisions made before they were used for the KJV were good, and all those made after were bad? On what grounds? Are we supposed to believe the translators always made the right choice when choosing between contradictory passages in the various editions? "We believe that God providentially guided them to make the correct choices." How do you know? Do you have a Bible verse to prove it? No! You are going by your own feelings based on nothing, or you are taking someone else's word for it (which means you have a man-made doctrine). Why is it that all revisions are fine up until 1611, but all after that are evil?

Honest KJV Only people should realize that most of the same arguments used for the KJV could be used for the NIV. I could say the people who composed the Greek text and the translators were providentially guided in the production of the NIV. I could prove it by quoting some verse about God promising to preserve His Word. Then when you disagreed with me I could accuse you of not believing in the preservation of God's Word. I could say you are denying the providential workings of God. I could call you a Bible denier or some of the terrible things Peter Ruckman, Texe Marrs, William Grady and Gail Riplinger call those who disagree with them.

We are told the KJV was translated from the Textus Receptus, also called the Majority Text. We are told these are the same. However, these differ from each other in at least a thousand places. The KJV was not based exclusively on any of them. The people who composed the Greek texts, and the translators of the KJV, had to engage in textual criticism just like the one who produced the NIV and the NASB. The manuscripts the KJV is based on are not as uniform and consistent as the KJV'ers would like for us to think.

We are told by the KJV Only proponents group that since the Majority Text has more manuscripts in it, we should always follow it. You have to assume the majority is always right for that argument to carry any weight. According to the Bible, the majority are on the wrong road. (Matt.7:13-14) The majority did not want to enter the promised land, only Joshua and Caleb. (Num. 13,14) The majority wanted to crucify Christ. So the majority is not an indicator of truth.

The early church fathers did not quote from the type text the KJV is founded on. They always quoted from the Alexandrian family of manuscripts. The Lord Jesus Christ quoted the exact wording of the Vaticanus and Sinaiticus manuscripts (the ones the KJV advocates hate) even when the wording differed from that of the Hebrew text. (Matthew 15:8-9; Luke 4:18-19) There is overwhelming evidence that the Alexandrian text was widely attested and well known in the early second century. This evidence has convinced Christian scholars around the world. The vast majority of conservative scholars for the past century have agreed that the Alexandrian text is the closest to the wording of the original documents. Peter Ruckman admits this when he tells us that all the fundamental Bible schools in the United States and Europe think the Alexandrian text is the best. (HANDBOOK OF MANUSCRIPT EVIDENCE, p. 20)

Ruckman also says that all the early manuscripts belong to the Alexandrian family, "leaving the Syrian text standing like a cold cat in the snow, with nothing but late manuscripts to support it." (HANDBOOK, p. 89)

The reason why the Majority text has more manuscripts in it is because it is newer. Common sense will tell you that more of the older manuscripts would disappear, and the newest ones would remain. As things get older, they disappear. For example: how many Model A Fords are there in existence today? How many modern cars stream along our highways? This principle applies to everything, including Bible manuscripts.

GOD HAS PROMISED TO PRESERVE HIS WORD.

Of course God has promised to preserve His word. I believe with all my heart that He not only promised it, He has done it. We have the preserved Word of God today. But I cannot see how this Bible truth applies to the KJV Only issue. God promises to preserve His Word, but He never promised it would be only in the KJV. You cannot show me any Scripture that says He will. God's Word is forever settled in Heaven. (Psalm 119:89) But that verse says nothing about the KJV. Psalm 12:6-7 tells us God will preserve His word, but He does not mention the KJV. The King James Version is not mentioned in Scripture. Therefore, if you say it is, you are adding to the Bible.

If the verses quoted above refer to the KJV, when someone read the Bible before 1611, how would they apply? We are asked to believe all the Bibles before the KJV were wrong, and all the Bibles after the KJV are wrong, but the KJV is right.

If anyone could prove a perfect English translation exists (which is impossible), they would still have to further prove that the KJV was it. Until they show me a verse that says, "Verily I say unto you, the KJV is God's perfect Word. Thou shall use it and no other." I will not be convinced.

The KJV supporters believe in Heaven. They can give Scripture to prove it. They believe in Hell and can give plenty of verses to prove it. They believe in the inspiration of Scripture and can prove it from the Bible. They believe in the preservation of God's

Word. They can give Scripture for it. They can give a string of verses for everything they believe. However, they cannot give one verse to prove the KJV is God's perfect Word for the English speaking people today. Yet they believe it so strongly. It is amazing that anyone could be so blind!

Here is another ridiculous contradiction among KJV Only proponents, who believe so strongly that God can and will preserve His Word. They are the very ones who are so concerned about God's Word being corrupted. Stop worrying, God will preserve His Word, just like He said.

CONCLUSION

Dear Reader, if you are not convinced yet, let me give one last call for honesty. Do you really believe the KJV translators were wrong when they said, "The meanest translation is the Word of God"? Were they wrong to say, "A variety of translations are necessary"? Will you actually say that "slew and hung on a tree" is better than "slew by hanging on a tree"? Do you really believe that Christ appeared "in the end of the world" is better than He appeared in the "end of the age"? Were all the great fundamentalists wrong? Have all the Christians down through church history been wrong? Was the vast majority of great scholars wrong until Peter Ruckman came along? Will you tell me it is better to have contradictions in the KJV than to have no contradictions in the NIV? Can you honestly say that all the obsolete words in the KJV are irrelevant? Do you suggest that one could never be misled by them? Do you really believe that all the outdated words and phrases are just as good for a new reader or a child, as the contemporary American English? Can you give one Scripture to prove your point (in context)? Do you believe what you believe because of the facts, or because you choose to believe? Did you make the decision yourself, or are you just following others you have confidence in? Honestly answer these questions. Do not dodge them, as is customary for KJV Only advocates.

Do you really believe God requires a new convert to read the KJV Only books before he would be qualified to pick out a Bible which would be the Word of God? In other words, what if a new

Christian walked into a Bible book store to get a Bible, and he picked at random one of the many translations, without knowing the differences in the many versions available today. The KJV Only advocates say it would not be the Word of God, but a perversion. Riplinger says it would be a book to help prepare him to receive the Anti-Christ. If the KJV Onlies are right, this new convert must be able to discern which family of manuscripts are good. He must know Westcott and Hort's texts are bad. Out of the dozens of English versions, he must be able pick the old KJV, in order to have the word of God. God never required this of new (or old) Christians in the past. Has God suddenly added a new requirement? I think not. I believe any version is the Word of God. However, it may not be the *best* translation.

I realize that some people will not be convinced, regardless of the facts. Their decision to be KJV Only was not based on facts, so the facts will not change their mind. Some are "willingly ignorant." (II Peter 3:5)

HERESY

Heresy is one of the works of the flesh mentioned in Gal. 5:19-22. The KJV Only doctrine appeals to the flesh. It requires no study. Their books are full of lies and slander. All of this is the works of the flesh and it has an appeal to certain people. It certainly is not built on the facts. All the years of extensive research by them has not produced one Scripture to prove their point, or one sound argument. All the books they write end up being a testimony against the KJV Only group.

All heresy is wicked and wrong. The KJV Only movement is worse because it divides God's people. This is a very serious sin. (Eph. 4:3) They spread slander and lies. The Bible says, "He that uttereth a slander, is a fool." (Proverbs 10:18) They restrict God's people from understanding His Word by withholding the good modern Bible versions. Comparing translations is one of the most profitable ways to study the Word. The KJV Only advocates deprive God's people of this help. Worst of all, the KJV Only group blasphemes God's word found in the Alexandrian Greek manuscripts and in other English versions. Please, dear reader, do not be a partaker of their evil deeds.

The KJV Only group has perverted the fundamental doctrine of the inspiration of the Scriptures. Christians have always believed the final authority was in the original writings. Now we are told the final authority is the King James Version. Thus they have changed and perverted this great basic doctrine of the Christian faith. This is a very serious wicked sin. The Bible remedy for sin is to repent and ask God for forgiveness.

APPENDIX
A

The Translators To The Readers
Preface to the King James Version 1611

Written by the King James Translators

The old English has been updated for readability.

Note: Page numbers listed on the following pages are the same as they appear in the 1611 King James Version of the Bible and do not reflect actually pages in this book.

THE TRANSLATORS TO THE READER

Preface to the King James Version 1611

Zeal to promote the common good, whether it be by devising anything ourselves, or revising that which hath been laboured by others, deserveth certainly much respect and esteem, but yet findeth but cold entertainment in the world. It is welcomed with suspicion instead of love, and with emulation instead of thanks: and if there be any hole left for cavil to enter, (and cavil, if it do not find a hole, will make one) it is sure to be misconstrued, and in danger to be condemned. This will easily be granted by as many as know story, or have any experience. For, was there ever any-projected, that savoured any way of newness or renewing, but the same endured many a storm of gainsaying, or opposition? A man would think that Civility, wholesome Laws, learning and eloquence, Synods, and Church-maintenance, (that we speak of no more things of this kind) should be as safe as a Sanctuary, and out of shot, as they say, that no man would lift up the heel, no, nor dog move his tongue against the motioners of them. For by the first, we are distinguished from brute beasts lead with sensuality; By the second, we are bridled and restrained from outrageous behaviour, and from doing of injuries, whether by fraud or by violence; By the third, we are enabled to inform and reform others, by the light and feeling that we have attained unto ourselves; Briefly, by the fourth being brought together to a parley face to face, we sooner compose our differences than by writings which are endless; And lastly, that the Church be sufficiently provided for, is so agreeable to good reason and conscience, that those mothers are holden to be less cruel, that kill their children as soon as they are born, than those nursing fathers and mothers (wheresoever they be) that withdraw from them who hang upon their breasts (and upon whose breasts again themselves do hang to receive the Spiritual and sincere milk of the word) livelihood and support fit for their estates. Thus it is apparent, that these things which we speak of, are of most necessary use, and therefore, that none, either without

absurdity can speak against them, or without note of
wickedness can spurn against them.

   Yet for all that, the learned know that certain worthy men
[Anacharsis with others] have been brought to untimely death
for none other fault, but for seeking to reduce their Countrymen
to god order and discipline; and that in some Commonwealths
[e.g. Locri] it was made a capital crime, once to motion the
making of a new Law for the abrogating of an old, though the
same were most pernicious; And that certain [Cato the elder],
which would be counted pillars of the State, and patterns of
Virtue and Prudence, could not be brought for a long time to give
way to good Letters and refined speech, but bare themselves as
averse from them, as from rocks or boxes of poison; And
fourthly, that he was no babe, but a great clerk [Gregory the
Divine], that gave forth (and in writing to remain to posterity)
in passion peradventure, but yet he gave forth, that he had not
seen any profit to come by any Synod, or meeting of the Clergy,
but rather the contrary; And lastly, against Church-
maintenance and allowance, in such sort, as the Ambassadors
and messengers of the great King of Kings should be furnished,
it is not unknown what a fiction or fable (so it is esteemed, and
for no better by the reporter himself [Nauclerus], though
superstitious) was devised; Namely, that at such a time as the
professors and teachers of Christianity in the Church of Rome,
then a true Church, were liberally endowed, a voice forsooth was
heard from heaven, saying: Now is poison poured down into the
Church, etc. Thus not only as oft as we speak, as one saith, but
also as oft as we do anything of note or consequence, we subject
ourselves to everyone's censure, and happy is he that is least
tossed upon tongues; for utterly to escape the snatch of them it
is impossible. If any man conceit, that this is the lot and portion
of the meaner sort only, and that Princes are privileged by their
high estate, he is deceived. "As the sword devoureth as well one
as the other," as it is in Samuel [2 Sam 11:25], nay as the great
Commander charged his soldiers in a certain battle, to strike at
no part of the enemy, but at the face; And as the King of Syria
commanded his chief Captains to "fight neither with small nor
great, save only against the King of Israel:" [1 Kings 22:31] so it

is too true, that Envy striketh most spitefully at the fairest, and at the chiefest. David was a worthy Prince, and no man to be compared to him for his first deeds, and yet for as worthy as act as ever he did (even for bringing back the Ark of God in solemnity) he was scorned and scoffed at by his own wife [2 Sam 6:16]. Solomon was greater than David, though

Page 2

not in virtue, yet in power: and by his power and wisdom he built a Temple to the Lord, such a one as was the glory of the land of Israel, and the wonder of the whole world. But was that his magnificence liked of by all? We doubt it. Otherwise, why do they lay it in his son's dish, and call unto him for easing the burden, "Make", say they, "the grievous servitude of thy father, and his sore yoke, lighter?" [1 Kings 12:4] Belike he had charged them with some levies, and troubled them with some carriages; Hereupon they raise up a tragedy, and wish in their heart the Temple had never been built. So hard a thing it is to please all, even when we please God best, and do seek to approve ourselves to every ones conscience.

If we will descend to later times, we shall find many the like examples of such kind, or rather unkind acceptance. The first Roman Emperor [C. Caesar, Plutarch] did never do a more pleasing deed to the learned, nor more profitable to posterity, for conserving the record of times in true supputation; than when he corrected the Calendar, and ordered the year according to the course of the Sun; and yet this was imputed to him for novelty, and arrogance, and procured to him great obloquy. So the first Christened Emperor [Constantine] (at the least-wise that openly professed the faith himself, and allowed others to do the like) for strengthening the Empire at his great charges, and providing for the Church, as he did, got for his labour the name Pupillus, as who would say, a wasteful Prince, that had need of a Guardian or overseer [Aurel. Victor]. So the best Christened Emperor [Theodosius], for the love that he bare unto peace, thereby to enrich both himself and his subjects, and because he did not see war but find it, was judged to be no man at arms

[Zosimus], (though indeed he excelled in feats of chivalry, and showed so much when he was provoked) and condemned for giving himself to his ease, and to his pleasure. To be short, the most learned Emperor of former times [Justinian], (at the least, the greatest politician) what thanks had he for cutting off the superfluities of the laws, and digesting them into some order and method? This, that he had been blotted by some to be an Epitomist, that is, one that extinguishes worthy whole volumes, to bring his abridgments into request. This is the measure that hath been rendered to excellent Princes in former times, even, *Cum bene facerent, male audire,* For their good deeds to be evil spoken of. Neither is there any likelihood, that envy and malignity died, and were buried with the ancient. No, no, the reproof of Moses taketh hold of most ages; "You are risen up in your fathers' stead, and increase of sinful men." [Num 32:14] "What is that that hath been done? that which shall be done; and there is no new thing under the Sun," saith the wiseman: [Ecc 1:9] and S. Stephen, "As your fathers did, so do you." [Acts 7:51] This, and more to this purpose, His Majesty that now reigneth (and long, and long may he reign, and his offspring forever, "Himself and children, and children's always) knew full well, according to the singular wisdom given unto him by God, and the rare learning and experience that he hath attained unto; namely that whosoever attempteth anything for the public (especially if it pertain to Religion, and to the opening and clearing of the word of God) the same setteth himself upon a stage to be gloated upon by every evil eye, yea, he casteth himself headlong upon pikes, to be gored by every sharp tongue. For he that medleth with men's Religion in any part, medleth with their custom, nay, with their freehold; and though they find no content in that which they have, yet they cannot abide to hear of altering. Notwithstanding his Royal heart was not daunted or discouraged for this that colour, but stood resolute, "as a statue immovable, and an anvil not easy to be beaten into plates," as one [Suidas] saith; he knew who had chosen him to be a Soldier, or rather a Captain, and being assured that the course which he intended made for the glory of God, and the building up of his Church, he would not suffer it to be broken off for whatsoever *speeches or practices. It doth certainly belong unto Kings, yea, it doth specially belong unto them, to have care of Religion, yea, it doth specially belong unto them, to have care of Religion, yea, to know it aright, yea, to profess it zealously, yea to promote it to the uttermost of their power. This is their glory before all nations which mean well, and this will bring unto them a far most excellent weight of glory in the day of the Lord Jesus. For the Scripture saith not in vain, "Them that honor me, I will honor." [1 Sam 2:30] neither was it a vain word that <u>Eusebius</u> delivered long ago, that piety towards God was the weapon and the only weapon, that both preserved Constantine's person, and avenged him of his enemies [Eusebius lib 10 cap 8].*

But now what piety without truth? what truth (what saving truth) without the word of God? What word of God (whereof we may be sure) without the Scripture? The Scriptures we are commanded to search. John 5:39. Isa 8:20. They are commended that searched and studied them. Acts 17:11 and 8:28,29. They are reproved that were unskillful in them, or slow to believe them. Matt 22:29. Luke 24:25. They can make us wise unto salvation. 2 Tim 3:15. If we be ignorant, they will instruct us; if out of the way, they will bring us home; if out of order, they will reform us; if in heaviness, comfort us; if dull, quicken us; if cold, inflame us. Tolle, lege; Tolle, lege, Take up and read, take up and read the Scriptures [S. August. confess. lib 8 cap 12], (for unto them was the direction) it was said unto S. Augustine by a supernatural voice. Whatsoever is in the Scriptures, believe me," saith the same S. Augustine, "is high and divine; there is verily truth, and a doctrine most fit for the refreshing of men's minds, and truly so tempered, that

everyone may draw from thence that which is sufficient for him, if he come to draw with a devout and pious mind, as true Religion requireth." [S. August. de utilitcredendi cap. 6] Thus S. Augustine, and S. Jerome: "Ama scripturas, et amabit te sapientia etc." [S. Jerome. ad Demetriad] Love the Scriptures, and wisdom will love thee. And S. Cyril against Julian; "Even boys that are bred up in the Scriptures, become most religious, etc." [S. Cyril. 7 contra Iulianum] But what mention we three or four uses of the Scripture, whereas whatsoever is to be believed or practiced, or hoped for, is contained in them? or three or four sentences of the Fathers, since whosoever is worthy the name of a Father, from Christ's time downward, hath likewise written not only of the riches, but also of the perfection of the Scripture? "I adore the fulness of the Scripture," saith Tertullian against Hermogenes. [Tertul. advers. Hermo.] And again, to Apelles an heretic of the like stamp, he saith; "I do not admit that which thou bringest in (or concludest) of thine own (head or store, de tuo) without Scripture." [Tertul. de carne Christi.] So Saint Justin Martyr before him; "We must know by all means," saith he, "that it is not lawful (or possible) to learn (anything) of God or of right piety, save only out of the Prophets, who teach us by divine inspiration." So Saint Basil after Tertullian, "It is a manifest falling way from the Faith, and a fault of presumption, either to reject any of those things that are written, or to bring in (upon the head of them) any of those things that are not written. We omit to cite to the same effect, S. Cyril B. of Jerusalem in his 4: Cataches., Saint Jerome against Helvidius, Saint Augustine in his 3::book against the letters of Petilian, and in very many other places of his works. Also we forebear to descend to later Fathers, because we will not weary the reader. The Scriptures then being acknowledged to be so full and so perfect, how can we excuse ourselves of negligence, if we do not study them, of curiosity, if we be not content with them? Men talk much of [an olive bow wrapped about with wood, whereupon did hang figs, and bread, honey in a pot, and oil], how many sweet and goodly things it had hanging on it; of the Philosopher's stone, that it turned copper into gold; of Cornucopia, that it had all things necessary for food in it, of Panaces the herb, that it was good for diseases, of Catholicon the drug, that it is instead of all purges; of Vulcan's armor, that it was an armor of proof against all thrusts, and all blows, etc. Well, that which they falsely or vainly attributed to these things for bodily god, we may justly and with full measure ascribe unto the Scripture, for spiritual. It is not only an armor, but also a whole armory of weapons, both offensive and defensive; whereby we may save ourselves and put the enemy to flight. It is not an herb, but a tree, or rather a whole paradise of trees of life, which bring forth fruit every month, and the fruit thereof is for meat, and the leaves for medicine. It is not a pot of Manna, or a cruse of oil, which were for memory only, or for a meal's meat or two, but as it were a shower of heavenly bread sufficient for a whole host, be it never so great; and as it were a whole cellar full of oil vessels; whereby all our necessities may be provided for, and our debts discharged. In a word, it is a Panary of wholesome food, against fenowed traditions; a Physician's shop (Saint Basil called it) [S. Basil in Psal. primum.] of preservatives against poisoned heresies; a Pandect of profitable laws, against rebellious spirits; a treasury of most costly jewels, against beggarly rudiments; finally a fountain of most pure water springing up unto everlasting life. And what marvel? *The original thereof being from heaven, not from earth; the author being God, not man; the inditer, the holy spirit, not the wit of the Apostles or Prophets;* the Penmen such as were sanctified from the womb, and endued with a principal portion of God's spirit; the matter, verity, piety, purity, uprightness; the form, God's word, God's testimony, God's oracles, the word of truth, the word of salvation, etc.; the effects, light of understanding, stableness of persuasion, repentance from dead works, newness of life, holiness, peace, joy in the holy Ghost; lastly, the end and reward of the study thereof, fellowship with the Saints, participation of the heavenly nature, fruition of an inheritance immortal, undefiled, and that never shall fade away: Happy is the man that delighted in the Scripture, and thrice happy that meditateth in it day and night.

But how shall men meditate in that, which they cannot understand? How shall they understand that which is kept close in an unknown tongue? as it is written, "Except I know the power of the voice, I shall be to him that speaketh, a Barbarian, and he that speaketh, shall be a Barbarian to me." [1 Cor 14] The Apostle excepteth no tongue; not Hebrew the ancientest, not Greek the most copious, not Latin the finest. Nature taught a natural man to confess, that all of us in those tongues which we

do not understand, are plainly deaf; we may turn the deaf ear
unto them. The Scythian counted the Athenian, whom he did
not understand, barbarous; [Clem. Alex. 1 Strom.] so the
Roman did the Syrian, and the Jew (even S. Jerome himself
called the Hebrew tongue barbarous, belike because it was
strange to so many) [S. Jerome. Damaso.] so the Emperor of
Constantinople [Michael. Theophili fil.] calleth the Latin tongue,
barbarous, though Pope Nicolas do storm at it: [2::Tom. Concil.
ex edit. Petri Crab] so the Jews long before Christ called all other
nations, Lognazim, which is little better than barbarous.
Therefore as one complaineth, that always in the Senate of
Rome, there was one or other that called for an interpreter:
[Cicero 5::de finibus.] so lest the Church be driven to the like
exigent, _it is necessary to have translations in a readiness._
Translation it is that openeth the window, to let in the light;
that breaketh the shell, that we may eat the kernel; that putteth
aside the curtain, that we may look into the most Holy place;
that removeth the cover of the well, that we may come by the
water, even as Jacob

rolled away the stone from the mouth of the well, by which
means the flocks of Laban were watered [Gen 29:10]. Indeed
without translation into the vulgar tongue, the unlearned are
but like children at Jacob's well (which is deep) [John 4:11]
without a bucket or something to draw with; or as that person
mentioned by Isaiah, to whom when a sealed book was delivered,
with this motion. "Read this, I pray thee," he was fain to make
this answer, _"I cannot, for it is sealed."_ [Isa 29:11]
      While God would be known only in Jacob, and have his
Name great in Israel, and in none other place, while the dew lay
on Gideon's fleece only, and all the earth besides was dry; then
for one and the same people, which spake all of them the
language of Canaan, that is, Hebrew, one and the same original
in Hebrew was sufficient. [S. August. lib 12 contra Faust c32]
But, when the fulness of time drew near, that the Sun of
righteousness, the Son of God should come into the world,

whom God ordained to be a reconciliation through faith in his blood, not of the Jew only, but also of the Greek, yea, of all them that were scattered abroad; then lo, it pleased the Lord to stir up the spirit of a Greek Prince (Greek for descent and language) even of Ptolemy Philadelph King of Egypt, to procure the translating of the _Book of God out of Hebrew into Greek. This is the translation of the Seventy Interpreters_, commonly so called, which prepared the way for our Saviour among the Gentiles by written preaching, as Saint John Baptist did among the Jews by vocal. For the Grecians being desirous of learning, were not wont to suffer books of worth to lie moulding in Kings' libraries, but had many of their servants, ready scribes, to copy them out, and so they were dispersed and made common. Again, the Greek tongue was well known and made familiar to most inhabitants in Asia, by reason of the conquest that there the Grecians had made, as also by the Colonies, which thither they had sent. For the same causes also it was well understood in many places of Europe, yea, and of Africa too. Therefore the word of God being set forth in Greek, becometh hereby like a candle set upon a candlestick, which giveth light to all that are in the house, or like a proclamation sounded forth in the market place, which most men presently take knowledge of; and therefore that language was fittest to contain the Scriptures, both for the first Preachers of the Gospel to appeal unto for witness, and for the learners also of those times to make search and trial by. _It is certain, that that Translation was not so sound and so perfect, but it needed in many places correction_; and who had been so sufficient for this work as the Apostles or Apostolic men? _Yet it seemed good to the holy Ghost and to them, to take that which they found, (the same being for the greatest part true and sufficient)_ rather than making a new, in that new world and green age of the Church, to expose themselves to many exceptions and cavillations, as though they made a Translations to serve their own turn, and therefore bearing a witness to themselves, their witness not to be regarded. This may be supposed to be some cause, why the Translation of the Seventy was allowed to pass for current. Notwithstanding, though it was commended generally, yet it did not fully content the learned, no not of the

Jews. For not long after Christ, Aquila fell in hand with a new Translation, and after him Theodotion, and after him Symmachus; yea, there was a fifth and a sixth edition, the Authors whereof were not known. [Epiphan. de mensur. et ponderibus.] These with the Seventy made up the Hexapla and were worthily and to great purpose compiled together by Origen. Howbeit the Edition of the Seventy went away with the credit, and therefore not only was placed in the midst by Origen (for the worth and excellency thereof above the rest, as Epiphanius gathered) but also was used by the Greek fathers for the ground and foundation of their Commentaries. Yea, Epiphanius above named doeth attribute so much unto it, that he holdeth the Authors thereof not only for Interpreters, but also for Prophets in some respect [S. August. 2::de dectrin. Christian c. 15]; and Justinian the Emperor enjoining the Jews his subjects to use especially the Translation of the Seventy, rendreth this reason thereof, because they were as it were enlightened with prophetical grace. Yet for all that, as the Egyptians are said of the Prophet to be men and not God, and their horses flesh and not spirit [Isa 31:3]; so it is evident, (and Saint Jerome affirmeth as much) [S. Jerome. de optimo genere interpret.] that the Seventy were Interpreters, they were not Prophets; they did many things well, as learned men; but yet as men they stumbled and fell, one while through oversight, another while through ignorance, yea, sometimes they may be noted to add to the Original, and sometimes to take from it; which made the Apostles to leave them many times, when they left the Hebrew, and to deliver the sense thereof according to the truth of the word, as the spirit gave them utterance. This may suffice touching the Greek Translations of the Old Testament.

There were also within a few hundred years after CHRIST, translations many into the Latin tongue: for this tongue also was very fit to convey the Law and the Gospel by, because in those times very many Countries of the West, yea of the South, East and North, spake or understood Latin, being made Provinces to the Romans. But now the Latin Translations were too many to be all good, for they were infinite (Latini Interprets nullo modo numerari possunt, saith S. Augustine.)

[S. Augustin. de doctr. Christ. lib 2 cap II]. Again they were not out of the Hebrew fountain (we speak of the Latin Translations of the Old Testament) but out of the Greek stream, therefore the Greek being not altogether clear, the Latin derived

Page 5

from it must needs be muddy. This moved S. Jerome a most learned father, and the best linguist without controversy, of his age, or of any that went before him, to undertake the translating of the Old Testament, out of the very fountain with that evidence of great learning, judgment, industry, and faithfulness, that he had forever bound the Church unto him, in a debt of special remembrance and thankfulness.

Now through the Church were thus furnished with Greek and Latin Translations, even before the faith of CHRIST was generally embraced in the Empire; (for the learned know that even in S. Jerome's time, the Consul of Rome and his wife were both Ethnics, and about the same time the greatest part of the Senate also) [S. Jerome. Marcell.Zosim] yet for all that the godly-learned were not content to have the Scriptures in the Language which they themselves understood, Greek and Latin, (as the good Lepers were not content to fare well themselves, but acquainted their neighbors with the store that God had sent, that they also might provide for themselves) [2 Kings 7:9] but also for the behoof and edifying of the unlearned which hungered and thirsted after righteousness, and had souls to be saved as well as they, they provided Translations into the vulgar for their Countrymen, insomuch that most nations under heaven did shortly after their conversion, hear CHRIST speaking unto them in their mother tongue, not by the voice of their Minister only, but also by the written word translated. If any doubt hereof, he may be satisfied by examples enough, if enough will serve the turn. First S. Jerome saith, Multarum gentium linguis Scriptura ante translata, docet falsa esse quae addita sunt, etc. i.e. "The Scripture being translated before in the languages of many Nations, doth show that those things that were added (by Lucian and Hesychius) are false." [S. Jerome. praef. in

4::Evangel.] So S. Jerome in that place. The same Jerome
elsewhere affirmeth that he, the time was, had set forth the
translation of the Seventy suae linguae hominibus, i.e., for his
countrymen of Dalmatia [S. Jerome. Sophronio.] Which words
not only Erasmus doth understand to purport, that S. Jerome
translated the Scripture into the Dalmatian tongue, but also
Sixtus Senensis [Six. Sen. lib 4], and Alphonsus a ` Castro
[Alphon. lb 1 ca 23] (that we speak of no more) men not to be
excepted against by them of Rome, do ingenuously confess as
much. So, S. Chrysostom that lived in S. Jerome's time, giveth
evidence with him: "The doctrine of S. John [saith he] did not in
such sort [as the Philosophers' did] vanish away: but the
Syrians, Egyptians, Indians, Persians, Ethiopians, and infinite
other nations being barbarous people translated it into their
[mother] tongue, and have learned to be [true] Philosophers." he
meaneth Christians. [S. Chrysost. in Johan. cap.I. hom.I.] To
this may be added Theodoret, as next unto him, both for
antiquity, and for learning. His words be these, "Every Country
that is under the Sun, is full of these words (of the Apostles and
Prophets) and the Hebrew tongue [he meaneth the Scriptures in
the Hebrew tongue] is turned not only into the Language of the
Grecians, but also of the Romans, and Egyptians, and Persians,
and Indians, and Armenians, and Scythians, and
Sauromatians, and briefly into all the Languages that any
Nation useth. [Theodor. 5. Therapeut.] So he. In like manner,
Ulfilas is reported by Paulus Diaconus and Isidor (and before
them by Sozomen) to have translated the Scriptures into the
Gothic tongue: [P. Diacon. li. 12.] John Bishop of Sevil by
Vasseus, to have turned them into Arabic, about the year of our
Lord 717; [Vaseus in Chron. Hispan.] Bede by Cistertiensis, to
have turned a great part of them into Saxon: Efnard by
Trithemius, to have abridged the French Psalter, as Beded had
done the Hebrew, about the year 800: King Alfred by the said
Cistertiensis, to have turned the Psalter into Saxon: [Polydor.
Virg. 5 histor.] Methodius by Aventinus (printed at Ingolstadt)
to have turned the Scriptures into Slavonian: [Aventin. lib. 4.]
Valdo, Bishop of Frising by Beatus Rhenanus, to have caused
about that time, the Gospels to be translated into Dutch

rhythm, yet extant in the Library of Corbinian: [Circa annum 900. B. Rhenan. rerum German. lib 2.] Valdus, by divers to have turned them himself into French, about the year 1160: Charles the Fifth of that name, surnamed the Wise, to have caused them to be turned into French, about 200 years after Valdus his time, of which translation there be many copies yet extant, as witnesseth Beroaldus. Much about that time, even in our King Richard the second's days, John Trevisa translated them into English, and many English Bibles in written hand are yet to be seen with divers, translated as it is very probable, in that age. So the Syrian translation of the New Testament is in most learned men's Libraries, of Widminstadius his setting forth, and the Psalter in Arabic is with many, of Augustinus Nebiensis' setting forth. So Postel affirmeth, that in his travel he saw the Gospels in the Ethiopian tongue; And Ambrose Thesius allegeth the Pslater of the Indians, which he testifieth to have been set forth by Potken in Syrian characters. So that, to have the Scriptures in the mother tongue is not a quaint conceit lately taken up, either by the Lord Cromwell in England, [Thuan.] or by the Lord Radevile in Polony, or by the Lord Ungnadius in the Emperor's dominion, but hath been thought upon, and put in practice of old, even from the first times of the conversion of any Nation; no doubt, because it was esteemed most profitable, to cause faith to grow in men's hearts the sooner, and to make them to be able to say with the words of the Psalms, "As we have heard, so we have seen." [Ps 48:8]

Now the Church of Rome would seem at the length to bear a motherly affection towards her children, and to allow them the Scriptures in their mother tongue: but indeed it is a gift, not deserving to be called a gift, an unprofitable gift: [Sophecles] they must first get a licence in writing before they may use

them, and to get that, they must approve themselves to their Confessor, that is, to be such as are, if not frozen in the dregs, yet soured with the leaven of their superstition. Howbeit, it seemed too much to Clement the Eighth that there should be any

Licence granted to have them in the vulgar tongue, and therefore
he overruleth and frustrateth the grant of Pius the Fourth. [See
the observation (set forth by Clemen. His authority) upon the 4.
rule of Pius the 4. his making in the index. lib. prohib. pag. 15.
ver. 5.] So much are they afraid of the light of the Scripture,
(Lucifugae Scripturarum, as Tertulian speaketh) that they will
not trust the people with it, no not as it is set forth by their own
sworn men, no not with the Licence of their own Bishops and
Inquisitors. Yea, so unwilling they are to communicate the
Scriptures to the people's understanding in any sort, that they
are not ashamed to confess, that we forced them to translate it
into English against their wills. This seemeth to argue a bad
cause, or a bad conscience, or both. Sure we are, that it is not he
that hath good gold, that is afraid to bring it to the touchstone,
but he that hath the counterfeit; [Tertul. de resur. carnis.]
neither is it the true man that shunneth the light, but the
malefactor, lest his deeds should be reproved [John 3:20]: neither
is it the plaindealing Merchant that is unwilling to have the
weights, or the meteyard brought in place, but he that useth
deceit. But we will let them alone for this fault, and return to
translation.

Many men's mouths have been open a good while (and yet
are not stopped) with speeches about the Translation so long in
hand, or rather perusals of Translations made before: and ask
what may be the reason, what the necessity of the employment:
Hath the Church been deceived, say they, all this while? Hath
her sweet bread been mingled with leaven, here silver with dross,
her wine with water, her milk with lime? (Lacte gypsum male
miscetur, saith S. Ireney.) [S. Iren. 3. lib. cap. 19.] We hoped
that we had been in the right way, that we had the Oracles of
God delivered unto us, and that though all the world had cause
to be offended and to complain, yet that we had none. Hath the
nurse holden out the breast, and nothing but wind in it? Hath
the bread been delivered by the fathers of the Church, and the
same proved to be lapidosus, as Seneca speaketh? What is it to
handle the word of God deceitfully, if this be not? Thus certain
brethren. Also the adversaries of Judah and Jerusalem, like
Sanballat in Nehemiah, mock, as we hear, both the work and

the workmen, saying; "What do these weak Jews, etc. will they make the stones whole again out of the heaps of dust which are burnt? although they build, yet if a fox go up, he shall even break down their stony wall." [Neh 4:3] Was their Translation good before? Why do they now mend it? Was it not good? Why then was it obtruded to the people? Yea, why did the Catholics (meaning Popish Romanists) always go in jeopardy, for refusing to go to hear it? Nay, if it must be translated into English, Catholics are fittest to do it. They have learning, and they know when a thing is well, they can manum de tabula. We will answer them both briefly: and the former, being brethren, thus, with S. Jerome, "Damnamus veteres? Mineme, sed post priorum studia in domo Domini quod possums laboramus." [S. Jerome, Apolog. advers. Ruffin.] That is, "Do we condemn the ancient? In no case: but after the endeavors of them that were before us, we take the best pains we can in the house of God." As if he said, Being provoked by the example of the learned men that lived before my time, I have thought it my duty, to assay whether my talent in the knowledge of the tongues, may be profitable in any measure to God's Church, lest I should seem to laboured in them in vain, and lest I should be thought to glory in men, (although ancient,) above that which was in them. Thus S. Jerome may be thought to speak.

And to the same effect say we, that we are so far off from condemning any of their labors that travailed before us in this kind, either in this land or beyond sea, either in King Henry's time, or King Edward's (if there were any translation, or correction of a translation in his time) or Queen Elizabeth's of ever renowned memory, that we acknowledge them to have been raised up of God, for the building and furnishing of his Church, and that they deserve to be had of us and of posterity in everlasting remembrance. The judgment of Aristotle is worthy and well known: "If Timotheus had not been, we had not had much sweet music; but if Phrynis [Timotheus his master] had not been, we had not had Timotheus." Therefore blessed be they, and most honoured be their name, that break the ice, and giveth onset upon that which helpeth forward to the saving of souls. Now what can be more available thereto, than to deliver God's

3.

4.

book unto God's people in a tongue which they understand?
Since of a hidden treasure, and of a fountain that is sealed,
there is no profit, as Ptolemy Philadelph wrote to the Rabbins or
masters of the Jews, as witnesseth Epiphanius: [S. Epiphan. loco
ante citato.] and as S. Augustine saith; "A man had rather be
with his dog than with a stranger (whose tongue is strange
unto him)." [S. Augustin. lib. 19. de civil. Dei. c. 7.] Yet for all
that, as nothing is begun and perfected at the same time, and
the later thoughts are thought to be the wiser: so, if we building
upon their foundation that went before us, and being holpen by
their labours, do endeavor to make that better which they left so
good; no man, we are sure, hath cause to mislike us; they, we
persuade ourselves, if they were alive, would thank us. The
vintage of Abienzer, that strake the stroke: yet the gleaning of
grapes of Ephraim was not to be despised. See Judges 8:2. Joash
the king of Israel did not satisfy himself, till he had smitten the
ground three times; and yet he offended the Prophet, for giving
over then. [2 Kings 13:18-19] Aquila, of whom we spake before,
translated

Page 7

the Bible as carefully, and as skilfully as he could; and yet he
thought good to go over it again, and then it got the credit with
the Jews, to be called accurately done, as Saint Jerome witnesseth.
[S. Jerome. in Ezech. cap. 3.] How many books of profane
learning have been gone over again and again, by the same
translators, by others? Of one and the same book of Aristotle's
Ethics, there are extant not so few as six or seven several
translations. Now if this cost may be bestowed upon the gourd,
which affordeth us a little shade, and which today flourisheth,
but tomorrow is cut down; what may we bestow, nay what
ought we not to bestow upon the Vine, the fruit whereof maketh
glad the conscience of man, and the stem whereof abideth
forever? And this is the word of God, which we translate.
"What is the chaff to the wheat, saith the Lord?" [Jer 23:28]
Tanti vitreum, quanti verum margaritum (saith Tertullian.)
[Tertul. ad Martyr.] if a toy of glass be of that reckoning with

5.

us, how ought we to value the true pearl? [Jerome. ad Salvin.]
Therefore let no man's eye be evil, because his Majesty's is good;
neither let any be grieved, that we have a Prince that seeketh the
increase of the spiritual wealth of Israel (let Sanballats and
Tobiahs do so, which therefore do bear their just reproof) but let
us rather bless God from the ground of our heart, for working
this religious care in him, <u>to have the translations of the Bible</u>
<u>maturely considered of and examined.</u> For by this means it
cometh to pass, that whatsoever is sound already (and all is
sound for substance, in one or other of our editions, and the
worst of ours far better than their authentic vulgar) the same
will shine as gold more brightly, being rubbed and polished;
also, <u>if anything be halting, or superfluous, or not so agreeable</u>
<u>to the original, the same may be corrected, and the truth set in</u>
<u>place.</u> And what can the King command to be done, that will
bring him more true honour than this? and wherein could they
that have been set a work, approve their duty to the King, yea
their obedience to God, and love to his Saints more, than by
yielding their service, and all that is within them, for the
furnishing of the work? But besides all this, they were the
principal motives of it, and therefore ought least to quarrel it:
for the very Historical truth is, that upon the importunate
petitions of the Puritans, at his Majesty's coming to this Crown,
the Conference at Hampton Court having been appointed for
hearing their complaints: when by force of reason they were put
from other grounds, they had recourse at the last, to this shift,
that they could not with good conscience subscribe to the
Communion book, since it maintained the Bible as it was there
translated, which was as they said, a most corrupted
translation. And although this was judged to be but a very poor
and empty shift; yet even hereupon did his Majesty begin to
bethink himself of the good that might ensue by a new
translation, and presently after gave order for this Translation
which is now presented unto thee. Thus much to satisfy our
scrupulous Brethren.

Now to the latter we answer; that we do not deny, <u>nay we</u>
<u>affirm and avow, that the very meanest translation of the Bible</u>
<u>in English</u>, set forth by men of our profession, (for we have seen

6.

none of theirs of the whole Bible as yet) containeth the word of God, nay, _is the word of God_. As the _King's speech_, which he uttereth in Parliament, being _translated_ into French, Dutch, Italian, and Latin, _is still the King's speech_, though it be not interpreted by every Translator with the like grace, nor peradventure so fitly for phrase, nor so expressly for sense, everywhere. For it is confessed, that things are to take their denomination of the greater part; and a natural man could say, Verum ubi multa nitent in carmine, non ego paucis offendor maculis, etc. [Horace.] _A man may be counted a virtuous man, though he have made many slips in his life, (else, there were none virtuous, for in many things we offend all) [James 3:2] also a comely man and lovely, though he have some warts upon his hand, yea, not only freckles upon his face, but also scars. No cause therefore why the word translated should be denied to be the word, or forbidden to be current, notwithstanding that some imperfections and blemishes may be noted in the setting forth of it._ For whatever was perfect under the Sun, where Apostles or Apostolic men, that is, men endued with an extraordinary measure of God's spirit, and privileged with the privilege of infallibility, had not their hand? The Romanists therefore in refusing to hear, and daring to burn the Word translated, did no less than despite the spirit of grace, from whom originally it proceeded, and whose sense and meaning, as well as man's weakness would enable, it did express. Judge by an example or two. Plutarch writeth, that after that Rome had been burnt by the Gauls, they fell soon to build it again: but doing it in haste, they did not cast the streets, nor proportion the houses in such comely fashion, as had been most slightly and convenient; [Plutarch in Camillo.] was Catiline therefore an honest man, or a good patriot, that sought to bring it to a combustion? or Nero a good Prince, that did indeed set it on fire? So, by the story of Ezra, and the prophecy of Haggai it may be gathered, that the _Temple built by Zerubbabel_ after the return from Babylon, _was by no means to be compared to the former built by Solomon_ (for they that remembered the former, wept when they considered the latter) [Ezra 3:12] notwithstanding, might this latter either have been abhorred and forsaken by the Jews, or profaned by the Greeks? *The like we are to think of Translations. The translation of the Seventy dissenteth from the Original in many places, neither doth it come near it, for perspicuity, gravity, majesty; yet which of the Apostles did condemn it?*

Page 8

Condemn it? *Nay, they used it,* (as it is apparent, and as Saint Jerome and most learned men do confess) which they would not have done, nor by their example of using it, so grace and commend it to the Church, *if it had been unworthy of the appellation and name of the word of God.* And whereas they urge for their second defence of their vilifying and abusing of the English Bibles, or some pieces thereof, which they meet with, for that heretics (forsooth) were the Authors of the translations, (heretics they call us by the same right that they call themselves Catholics, both being wrong) we marvel what divinity taught them so. We are sure Tertullian was of another mind: Ex personis probamus fidem, an ex fide personas? [Tertul. de praescript. contra haereses.] Do we try men's faith by their persons? we should try their persons by their faith. Also S. *Augustine* was of another mind: for he lighting upon certain rules made by Tychonius a Donatist, for the better understanding of the word, was not ashamed to make use of them, yea, to insert them into his own book, *with giving commendation to them so far forth as they were worthy to be commended,* as is to be seen in S. Augustine's third book De doctrina Christiana. [S. August. 3. de doct. Christ. cap. 30.] To be short, Origen, and the whole Church of God for certain hundred years, were of another mind: for they were so far from treading under foot, (much more from burning) the Translation of Aquila a Proselyte, that is, one that had turned Jew; of Symmachus, and Theodotion, both Ebionites, that is, most vile heretics, that they joined together with the Hebrew Original, and the Translation of the Seventy (as hath been before signified out of Epiphanius) and set them forth openly to be considered of and perused by all. *But we weary the unlearned,* who need not know so much, and trouble *the learned, who know it already.*

Yet before we end, _we must answer a third cavil and objection_ _of theirs against us, for altering and amending our Translations_ _so oft;_ wherein truly they deal hardly, and strangely with us. For _to whomever was it imputed for a fault_ (by such as were wise) _to go over that which he had done, and to amend it where_ _he saw cause?_ Saint Augustine was not afraid to exhort S. Jerome to a Palinodia or recantation; [S. Aug. Epist. 9.] and doth even glory that he seeth his infirmities. [S. Aug. Epist. 8.] If we be sons of the Truth, we must consider what it speaketh, and trample upon our own credit, yea, and upon other men's too, if either be any way an hindrance to it. This to the cause: then to the persons we say, that of all men they ought to be most silent in this case. For what varieties have they, and what alterations have they made, not only of their Service books, Portesses and Breviaries, but also of their Latin Translation? The Service book supposed to be made by S. Ambrose (Officium Ambrosianum) was a great while in special use and request; but Pope Hadrian calling a Council with the aid of Charles the Emperor, abolished it, yea, burnt it, and commanded the Service book of Saint Gregory universally to be used. [Durand. lib. 5. cap. 2.] Well, Officium Gregorianum gets by this means to be in credit, but doth it continue without change or altering? No, the very Roman Service was of two fashions, the New fashion, and the Old, (the one used in one Church, the other in another) as is to be seen in Pamelius a Romanist, his Preface, before Micrologus. the same Pamelius reporteth out Radulphus de Rivo, that about the year of our Lord, 1277, Pope Nicolas the Third removed out of the Churches of Rome, the more ancient books (of Service) and brought into use the Missals of the Friers Minorites, and commanded them to be observed there; insomuch that about an hundred years after, when the above name Radulphus happened to be at Rome, he found all the books to be new, (of the new stamp). Neither were there this chopping and changing in the more ancient times only, but also of late: Pius Quintus himself confesseth, that every Bishopric almost had a peculiar kind of service, most unlike to that which others had: which moved him to abolish all other Breviaries, though never so ancient, and privileged and published by Bishops in their

Dioceses, and to establish and ratify that only which was of his own setting forth, in the year 1568. Now when the father of their Church, who gladly would heal the sore of the daughter of his people softly and slightly, and make the best of it, findeth so great fault with them for their odds and jarring; we hope the children have no great cause to vaunt of their uniformity. _But the difference that appeareth between our Translations, and our often correcting of them, is the thing that we are specially charged with;_ let us see therefore whether they themselves be without fault this way, (if it be to be counted a fault, to correct) and whether they be fit men to throw stones at us: O tandem maior parcas insane minori: they that are less sound themselves, out not to object infirmities to others. [Horat.] If we should tell them that Valla, Stapulensis, Erasmus, and Vives found fault with their vulgar Translation, and consequently wished the same to be mended, or a new one to be made, they would answer peradventure, that we produced their enemies for witnesses against them; albeit, they were in no other sort enemies, than as S. Paul was to the Galatians, for telling them the truth [Gal 4:16]: and it were to be wished, that they had dared to tell it them plainlier and oftener. But what will they say to this, that Pope Leo the Tenth allowed Erasmus' Translation of the New Testament, so much different from the vulgar, by his Apostolic Letter and Bull; that the same Leo exhorted Pagnine to translate the whole Bible.

Page 9

and bare whatsoever charges was necessary for the work? [Sixtus Senens.] Surely, as the Apostle reasoneth to the Hebrews, that if the former Law and Testament had been sufficient, there had been no need of the latter: [Heb 7:11 and 8:7] so we may say, that if the old vulgar had been at all points allowable, to small purpose had labour and charges been undergone, about framing of a new. If they say, it was one Pope's private opinion, and that he consulted only himself; then we are able to go further with them, and to aver, that more of their chief men of all sorts, even their own Trent champions Paiva and Vega, and

their own Inquisitors, Hieronymus ab Oleastro, and their own
Bishop Isidorus Clarius, and their own Cardinal Thomas a Vio
Caietan, do either make new Translations themselves, or follow
new ones of other men's making, or note the vulgar Interpreter
for halting; none of them fear to dissent from him, nor yet to
except against him. And call they this an uniform tenor of text
and judgment about the text, so many of their Worthies
disclaiming the now received conceit? Nay, we will yet come
nearer the quick: doth not their Paris edition differ from the
Lovaine, and Hentenius his from them both, and yet all of them
allowed by authority? Nay, doth not Sixtus Quintus confess,
that certain Catholics (he meaneth certain of his own side) were
in such an humor of translating the Scriptures into Latin, that
Satan taking occasion by them, though they thought of no such
matter, did strive what he could, out of so uncertain and
manifold a variety of Translations, so to mingle all things, that
nothing might seem to be left certain and firm in them, etc.?
[Sixtus 5. praefat. fixa Bibliis.] Nay, further, did not the same
Sixtus ordain by an inviolable decree, and that with the counsel
and consent of his Cardinals, that the Latin edition of the old
and new Testament, which the Council of Trent would have to
be authentic, is the same without controversy which he then set
forth, being diligently corrected and printed in the Printinghouse
of Vatican? Thus Sixtus in his Preface before his Bible. And yet
Clement the Eighth his immediate successor, published another
edition of the Bible, containing in it infinite differences from that
of Sixtus, (and many of them weighty and material) and yet
this must be authentic by all means. What is to have the faith
of our glorious Lord JESUS CHRIST with Yea or Nay, if this be
not? Again, what is sweet harmony and consent, if this be?
Therefore, as Demaratus of Corinth advised a great King,
before he talked of the dissensions of the Grecians, to compose
his domestic broils (for at that time his Queen and his son and
heir were at deadly feud with him) so all the while that our
adversaries do make so many and so various editions
themselves, and do jar so much about the worth and authority
of them, they can with no show of equity challenge us for
changing and correcting.

But it is high time to leave them, and to show in brief what we proposed to ourselves, and what course we held in this our perusal and survey of the Bible. _Truly (good Christian Reader) we never thought from the beginning, that we should need to make a new Translation, nor yet to make of a bad one a good one,_ (for then the imputation of Sixtus had been true in some sort, that our people had been fed with gall of Dragons instead of wine, with whey instead of milk:_) but to make a good one better, or out of many good ones, one principal good one,_ not justly to be excepted against; that hath been our endeavor, that our mark. To that purpose there were many chosen, that were greater in other men's eyes than in their own, and that sought the truth rather than their own praise. Again, they came or were thought to come to the work, not _exercendi causa_ (as one saith) but _exercitati,_ that is, learned, not to learn: For the chief overseer and [NOTE: Greek letters omitted] under his Majesty, to whom not only we, but also our whole Church was much bound, knew by his wisdom, which thing also Nazianzen taught so long ago, that it is a preposterous order to teach first and to learn after, yea that [NOTE: Greek letters omitted] to learn and practice together, is neither commendable for the workman, nor safe for the work. [_Idem in Apologet._] Therefore such were thought upon, as could say modestly with Saint Jerome, _Et Hebreaeum Sermonem ex parte didicimus, et in Latino pene ab ipsis incunabulis etc. detriti sumus._ "Both we have learned the Hebrew tongue in part, and in the Latin we have been exercised almost from our very cradle." S. Jerome maketh no mention of the Greek tongue, wherein yet he did excel, because he translated not the old Testament out of Greek, but out of Hebrew. And in what sort did these assemble? In the trust of their own knowledge, or of their sharpness of wit, or deepness of judgment, as it were in an arm of flesh? At no hand. They trusted in him that hath the key of David, opening and no man shutting; they prayed to the Lord the Father of our Lord, to the effect that S. Augustine did; "O let thy Scriptures be my pure delight, let me not be deceived in them, neither let me deceive by them." [_S. Aug. lib. II. Confess. cap. 2._] In this confidence, and with this devotion did they assemble together; not too many, lest one should trouble another; and yet many, lest many things haply might escape them. If you ask what they had before them, truly it was the Hebrew text of the Old Testament, the Greek of the New. These are the two golden pipes, or rather conduits, where-through the olive branches empty themselves into the gold. Saint Augustine calleth them precedent, _or original tongues_; [S. August. 3. de doctr. c. 3. etc.] Saint Jerome, fountains. [S. Jerome. ad Suniam et Fretel.] The same Saint Jerome affirmeth. [S. Jerome. ad Lucinium. Dist. 9 ut veterum.] and Gratian hath not spared to put it into his Decree, That "as the credit of the old Books" (he meaneth of the Old Testament) "_is to be tried by the_

Hebrew Volumes, so of the New by the Greek tongue," he _meaneth by the original Greek. If truth be tried by these tongues, then whence should a Translation be made, but out of them?_ These tongues therefore, the Scriptures we say in those tongues, we set before us to translate, _being the tongues wherein God was pleased to speak to his Church by the Prophets and Apostles._ Neither did we run over the work with that posting haste that the Septuagint did, if that be true which is reported of them, that they finished it in 72 days; [Joseph. Antiq. lib. 12.] _neither were we barred or hindered from going over it again, having once done it,_ like S. Jerome, if that be true which himself reporteth, that he could no sooner write anything, but presently it was caught from him, and published, and he could not have leave to mend it: [S. Jerome. ad Pammac. pro libr. advers. Iovinian.] neither, to be short, were we the first that fell in hand with translating the Scripture into English, and consequently destitute of former helps, as it is written of Origen, that he was the first in a manner, that put his hand to write Commentaries upon the Scriptures, [Sophoc. in Elect.] and therefore no marvel, if he overshot himself many times. None of these things: the work hath not been huddled up in 72 days, but hath cost the workmen, as light as it seemeth, the pains of twice seven times seventy two days and more: matters of such weight and *consequence are to be speeded with maturity: for in a business of movement a man feareth not the blame of convenient slackness. [S. Chrysost. in II. Thess. cap. 2.] Neither did we think much to consult the Translators or Commentators, Chaldee, Hebrew, Syrian, Greek or Latin, no nor the Spanish, French, Italian, or Dutch; neither did we disdain to revise that which we had done, and to bring back to the anvil that which we had hammered: but having and using as great helps as were needful, and fearing no reproach for slowness, nor coveting praise for expedition, we have at length, through the good hand of the Lord upon us, brought the work to that pass that you see.*

Some peradventure would have no variety of senses to be set in the margin, lest the authority of the Scriptures for deciding of controversies by that show of uncertainty, should somewhat be shaken. But we hold their judgment not to be sound in this point. For though, "whatsoever things are necessary are manifest," as S. Chrysostom saith, [S. Chrysost. in II. Thess. cap. 2.] and as S. Augustine, "In those things that are plainly set down in the Scriptures, all such matters are found that concern Faith, Hope, and Charity." [S. Aug. 2. de doctr. Christ. cap. 9.] Yet for all that it cannot be dissembled, that partly to exercise and whet our wits, partly to wean the curious from the loathing of them for their everywhere plainness, partly also to stir up our devotion to crave the assistance of God's spirit by prayer, and lastly, that we might be forward to seek aid of our brethren by conference, and never scorn those that be not in all respects so complete as they should be, being to seek in many things ourselves, it hath pleased God in his divine providence, here and there to scatter words and sentences of that difficulty and doubtfulness, not in doctrinal points that concern salvation, (for in such it hath been vouched that the Scriptures are plain) but in matters of less moment, that fearfulness would better beseem us than confidence, and if we will resolve upon modesty with S. Augustine, (though not in this same case altogether, yet upon the same ground) Melius est debitare de occultis, quam litigare de incertis, [S. Aug li. S. de Genes. ad liter. cap. 5.] "it is better to make doubt of those things which are secret, than to strive about those things that

12.

are uncertain." There be many words in the Scriptures, which be never found there but once, (having neither brother or neighbor, as the Hebrews speak) so that we cannot be holpen by conference of places. Again, there be many rare names of certain birds, beasts and precious stones, etc. concerning the Hebrews themselves are so divided among themselves for judgment, that they may seem to have defined this or that, rather because they would say something, than because they were sure of that which they said, as S. Jerome somewhere saith of the Septuagint. Now in such a case, doth not a margin do well to admonish the Reader to seek further, and _not to conclude or dogmatize upon this or that peremptorily?_ For as it is a fault of incredulity, to doubt of those things that are evident: so to determine _of such things as the Spirit of God hath left_ (even in the judgment of the judicious) _questionable,_ can be no less than presumption. Therefore as S. Augustine saith, _that variety of Translations is profitable for the finding out of the sense of the Scriptures:_ [S. Aug. 2. De doctr. Christian. cap. 14.] so diversity of signification and sense in the margin, _where the text is no so clear, must needs do good, yea, is necessary, as we are persuaded._ We know that Sixtus Quintus expressly forbiddeth, _that any variety of readings of their vulgar edition, should be put in the margin._ [Sixtus 5. praef. Bibliae.] (which though it be not altogether the same thing to that we have in hand, yet it looketh that way) but we think he hath not all of his own side his favorers, for this conceit. _They that are wise, had rather have their judgments at liberty in differences of readings, than to be captivated to one, when it may be the other._ If they were sure that their high Priest had all laws shut up in his breast, as Paul the Second bragged. [Plat. in Paulo secundo.] and that he were as free from error by special privilege, as the Dictators of Rome were made by law inviolable, it were another matter; then his word were an Oracle, his opinion a decision. But the eyes of the world are now open, God be thanked, and have been a great while, they find that _he is subject to the same affections and infirmities that others be, that his skin is penetrable,_ and therefore so much as he proveth, not as much as he claimeth, they grant and embrace.

13.

An other things we think good to admonish thee of (gentle
Reader) that we have not tied ourselves to an uniformity of
phrasing, or to an identity of words, as some peradventure
would wish that we had done, because they observe, that some
learned men somewhere, have been as exact as they could that
way. Truly, that we might not vary from the sense of that
which we had translated before, if the word signified that same
in both places (for there be some words that be not the same
sense everywhere) we were especially careful, and made a
conscience, according to our duty. <u>But, that we should express
the same notion in the same particular word</u>; as for example, if
we translate the Hebrew or Greek word once by *PURPOSE*,
never to call it *INTENT*; if one where *JOURNEYING*, never
TRAVELING; if one where *THINK*, never *SUPPOSE*; if one
where *PAIN*, never *ACHE*; if one where *JOY*, never *GLADNESS*,
etc. Thus to mince the matter, we thought to savour more of
curiosity than wisdom, and that rather it would breed scorn in
the Atheist, than bring profit to the godly Reader. <u>For is the
kingdom of God to become words or syllables?</u> why should we be
in bondage to them if we may be free, use one precisely when we
may use another no less fit, as commodiously? A godly Father in
the Primitive time showed himself greatly moved, that one of
newfangledness called [NOTE: Greek omitted but was a dispute
over the word for "a bed"] [Niceph. Calist. lib.8. cap.42.] though
the difference be little or none; and another reporteth that he
was much abused for turning "Cucurbita" (to which reading the
people had been used) into "Hedera". [S. Jerome in 4. Ionae. See
S. Aug: epist. 10.] Now if this happens in better times, and
upon so small occasions, we might justly fear hard censure, if
generally we should make verbal and unnecessary changings.
We might also be charged (by scoffers) with some unequal
dealing towards a great number of good English words. For as
it is written of a certain great Philosopher, that he should say ,
that those logs were happy that were made images to be
worshipped; for their fellows, as good as they, lay for blocks
behind the fire: so if we should say, as it were, unto certain

words. Stand up higher, have a place in the Bible always, and to others of like quality, Get ye hence, be banished forever, we might be taxed peradventure with S. James his words, namely, "To be partial in ourselves and judges of evil thoughts." Add hereunto, that niceness in words was always counted the next step to trifling, and so was to be curious about names too: also that we cannot follow a better pattern for elocution than God himself; therefore he using divers words, in his holy writ, and indifferently for one thing in nature: [see Euseb. li. 12. ex Platon.] we, if we will not be superstitious, may use the same liberty in our English versions out of Hebrew and Greek, for that copy or store that he hath given us. Lastly, <u>we have on the one side avoided the scrupulosity of the Puritans, who leave the old Ecclesiastical words</u>, and betake them to other, as when they put <u>WASHING for BAPTISM</u>, and CONGREGATION instead of CHURCH: as also on the other side we have shunned the obscurity of the Papists, in their AZIMES, TUNIKE, RATIONAL, HOLOCAUSTS, PRAEPUCE, PASCHE, and a number of such like, whereof their late Translation is full, and that of purpose to darken the sense, that since they must needs translate the Bible, yet by the language thereof, it may be kept from being understood. But we desire that the Scripture may speak like itself, as in the language of Canaan, <u>that it may be understood even of the very vulgar.</u>

   <u>Many other things we might give thee warning of (gentle Reader)</u> if we had not exceeded the measure of a Preface already. It remaineth, that we commend thee to God, and to the Spirit of his grace, which is able to build further than we can ask or think. He removeth the scales from our eyes, the vail from our hearts, opening our wits that we may understand his word, enlarging our hearts, yea correcting our affections, that we may love it to the end. Ye are brought unto fountains of living water which ye digged not; do not cast earth into them with the Philistines, neither prefer broken pits before them with the wicked Jews. [Gen 26:15. Jer 2:13.] Others have laboured, and you may enter into their labours; O receive not so great things in vain, O despise not so great salvation! Be not like swine to tread under foot so precious things, neither yet like dogs to tear and

*abuse holy things. Say not to our Saviour with the Gergesites,
Depart out of our coast [Matt 8:34]; neither yet with Esau sell
your birthright for a mess of pottage [Heb 12:16]. If light be
come into the world, love not darkness more than light; if food,
if clothing be offered, go not naked, starve not yourselves.
Remember the advice of Nazianzene, "It is a grievous thing" (or
dangerous) "to neglect a great fair, and to seek to make markets
afterwards:" also the encouragement of S. Chrysostom, "It is
altogether impossible, that he that is sober" (and watchful)
"should at any time be neglected:" [S. Chrysost. in epist. ad
Rom. cap. 14. oral. 26.] Lastly, the admonition and menacing of
S. Augustine, "They that despise God's will inviting them, shall
feel God's will taking vengeance of them." [S. August. ad artic.
sibi falso object. Artic. 16.] It is a fearful thing to fall into the
hands of the living God; [Heb 10:31] but a blessed thing it is,
and will bring us to everlasting blessedness in the end, when God
speaketh unto us, to hearken; when he setteth his word before
us, to read it; when he stretcheth out his hand and calleth, to
answer, Here am I, here we are to do thy will, O God. The Lord
work a care and conscience in us to know him and serve him,
that we may be acknowledged of him at the appearing of our
Lord Jesus Christ, to whom with the holy Ghost, be all praise
and thanksgiving. Amen.*

Below is a sample page from an original 1611 **KING JAMES VERSION BIBLE.** This is the **Gothic type**

come in a day when hee looketh not for him, and at an houre when hee is not ware, and will cut him in sunder, and will appoint him his portion with the vnbeleeuers.

Or, cut him off.

47 And that seruant which knew his Lords will, and prepared not himselfe, neither did according to his will, shalbe beaten with many stripes.

48 But hee that knew not, and did commit things worthy of stripes, shall be beaten with few stripes. For vnto whomsoeuer much is giuen, of him shall bee much required: and to whom men haue committed much, of him they will aske the more.

49 ¶ I am come to send fire on the earth, and what will I, if it be already kindled?

Or, pained.

50 But I haue a baptisme to be baptized with, and how am I straitned till it be accomplished?

Matt. 10. 34.

51 Suppose yee that I am come to giue peace on earth? I tell you, Nay, but rather diuision.

52 For from henceforth there shalbe fiue in one house diuided, three against two, and two against three.

53 The father shall bee diuided against the sonne, and the sonne against the father: the mother against the daughter, and the daughter against the mother: the mother in lawe against her daughter in lawe, and the daughter in law against her mother in law.

Math. 16. 2.

54 ¶ And he said also to the people, When yee see a cloud rise out of the west, straightway ye say, There commeth a showre, and so it is.

55 And when ye see the Southwind blow, ye say, There will be heat, and it commeth to passe.

56 Ye hypocrites, ye can discerne the face of the skie, and of the earth: but how is it that yee doe not discerne this time?

Math. 5. 25.

57 Yea, and why euen of your selues iudge ye not what is right?

58 ¶ When thou goest with thine aduersary to the magistrate, as thou art in the way, giue diligence that thou mayest be deliuered from him, lest hee hale thee to the Iudge, and the Iudge deliuer thee to the officer, and the officer cast thee into prison.

See Mat. 11.41.

59 I tell thee, Thou shalt not depart thence, till thou hast payd the very last mite.

CHAP. XIII.

1 Christ preacheth repentance vpon the punishment of the Galileans, and others. 6 The fruitlesse figge tree may not stand. 11 Hee healeth the crooked woman: 18 sheweth the powerfull working of the word in the hearts of his chosen, by the parable of the graine of mustard seed, and of leuen: 24 exhorteth to enter in at the strait gate, 31 and reproueth Herode, and Hierusalem.

There were present at that season, some that told him of the Galileans, whose blood Pilate had mingled with their sacrifices.

2 And Iesus answering, said vnto them, Suppose ye that these Galileans were sinners aboue all the Galileans, because they suffered such things?

3 I tell you, Nay: but except ye repent, ye shall all likewise perish.

4 Or those eighteene, vpon whom the towre in Siloe fell, and slew them, thinke ye that they were sinners aboue all men that dwelt in Hierusalem?

Or, debters.

5 I tell you, Nay: but except ye repent, ye shall all likewise perish.

6 ¶ Hee spake also this parable, A certaine man had a figge tree planted in his vineyard, and he came and sought fruit thereon, and found none.

7 Then said hee vnto the dresser of his vineyard, Beholde, these three yeeres I come seeking fruit on this figtree, and finde none: cut it downe, why cumbreth it the ground?

8 And he answering, said vnto him, Lord, let it alone this yeere also, till I shall digge about it, and doung it:

9 And if it beare fruit, well: and if not, then after that, thou shalt cut it downe.

10 And hee was teaching in one of the Synagogues on the Sabbath.

11 ¶ And beholde, there was a woman which had a spirit of infirmitie eighteene yeeres, and was bowed together, and could in no wise lift vp her selfe.

12 And when Iesus saw her, he called her to him, and said vnto her, Woman, thou art loosed from thy infirmitie.

13 And hee layed his handes on her, and immediatly shee was made straight, and glorified God.

14 And the ruler of the Synagogue answered with indignation, because that Iesus had healed on the Sabbath day,

Eptuagefima
Sexagefima } before Eafter { ix
Quinquagefima viij } weekes.
Quadragefima vij
vj

Ogations
Whitfunday } after Eafter { v
Trinitie Sunday vij } weekes.
viij

❧ Thefe to be obferued for Holy
dayes, and none other.

That is to fay : All Sun-
dayes in the yeere.
The dayes of the feafts
of the Circumcifion of our
Lord Jefus Chrift.
Of the Epiphanie.
Of the Purification of the bleffed
Virgin.
Of Saint Matthias the Apoftle.
Of the Annunciation of the bleffed
Virgin.
Of Saint Marke the Euangelift.
Of S. Philip and Jacob the Apo-
ftles.
Of the Afcenfion of our Lord Jefus
Chrift.
Of the Natiuity of Saint John
Baptift.

Of S. Peter the Apoftle.
Of S. James the Apoftle.
Of S. Bartholomew the Apoftle.
Of S. Matthew the Apoftle.
Of S. Michael the Archangel.
Of S. Luke the Euangelift.
Of S. Simon & Jude the Apofties.
Of All Saints.
Of S. Andrew the Apoftle.
Of S. Thomas the Apoftle.
Of the Natiuitie of our Lord.
Of S. Steuen the Martyr.
Of S. John the Euangelift.
Of the Holy Innocents.
Munday and Tuefday in Eafter
weeke.
Munday and Tuefday in Whitfun
weeke.

¶ The

Notes

Notes